NAZI WOMEN
OF THE
THIRD REICH

NAZI WOMEN
OF THE
THIRD REICH
SERVING THE SWASTIKA

PAUL ROLAND

ARCTURUS

ARCTURUS

This edition published in 2018 by Arcturus Publishing Limited
26/27 Bickels Yard, 151–153 Bermondsey Street,
London SE1 3HA

ISBN: 978-1-78828-082-2
AD005918UK

Printed in China

Contents

Introduction   7

Chapter One: **Paula, Hitler's Sister**   11

Chapter Two: **Hitler and the Braun Sisters**   18

Chapter Three: **Hitler's Female Admirers**   31

Chapter Four: **The Dove and the Eagle - Hitler's Valkyries** 47

Chapter Five: **Hitler's Jewish Princess**   85

Chapter Six: **Adolf's Eyes and Ears - Spying for Hitler**   97

Chapter Seven: **SS Wives**   115

Chapter Eight: **Women Behind the Wire**   124

Chapter Nine: **A Monster is Brought to Justice**   141

Chapter Ten: **Living with the Reich**   153

Chapter Eleven: **Growing Up Under Hitler**   167

Chapter Twelve: **Making a Stand**   180

Chapter Thirteen: **Doves and Eagles - the BDM**   192

Chapter Fourteen: **Swelling the Ranks**   203

Chapter Fifteen: **Women as Bringers of Death**   212

Chapter Sixteen: **Child Soldiers**   224

Bibliography   235

Index   237

Introduction

In a previous book, *Nazi Women* (Arcturus 2014), I questioned what lay behind the common perception of women in Nazi Germany as having been adoring acolytes of their false messiah Adolf Hitler, sadistic concentration camp guards or the callous, clinical functionaries who facilitated the process of mass murder.

In this book, I dig deeper to reveal the diversity of personalities who lived under one of the most repressive and barbarous regimes in modern history.

I have uncovered an extremely rare interview with Hitler's sister Paula, conducted by American Intelligence just a year after the war, in which she paints an idealized picture of their early life. She recalls her brother as being 'cheerful' but quarrelsome, a man 'radiant with kindness', and yet fails to see that her description of domestic bliss is irreconcilable with her admission to having been repeatedly subjected to his violent temper and 'felt his loose hand'.

I have also drawn upon rarely seen interviews with Eva Braun's sister Gretl and their cousin Gertrude Weisker, which are equally revealing and provide details regarding the relationship between Hitler and his mistress that have not, to my knowledge, been quoted elsewhere.

Hitler's mystifying attraction for women is highlighted in brief extracts from dozens of private letters written by his female followers, from the earliest days of the Party to the final weeks of the regime. These suggest that many of his most ardent admirers chose to see him as the 'strong man' that Germany needed at a time of political instability and uncertainty and that they projected on to him their hopes as well as their prejudices.

In Chapter Four, I consider the contrasting personalities of two extraordinary women, test pilots Hanna Reitsch and Melitta von Stauffenberg. Both were awarded the Iron

Cross for their courage and became symbols of the new Germany, but while Hanna chose to ally herself with the regime Melitta loathed the dictatorship that her husband's family would attempt to bring down. She justified her work for the Luftwaffe as being directed towards saving pilot's lives.

Equally charismatic was Princess Stephanie von Hohenlohe-Waldenburg-Schillingsfürst, an Austrian aristocrat and confidante of the Führer who became a high-profile pawn in the diplomatic game of bluff and brinkmanship that Hitler was playing out on the eve of the war, a role that is all the more remarkable given that she was Jewish – and Hitler knew it.

Princess Stephanie was among those whose activities captured the headlines in the interwar years, but there were many others who worked tirelessly against the regime in secret, such as the novelist Hildegard Kuhn, who returned to Germany in 1940 after faking her own death so that she could write about life under a dictatorship from the inside.

At the other end of the scale were those women who willingly chose to work for the Nazi cause, such as Annette Wagner, Violette Morris, Lilly Stein and Mildred Gillars (aka 'Axis Sally'), as either spies or purveyors of insidious propaganda. All had their reasons.

Psychopaths such as Hermine Braunsteiner, wife of the leader of an SS extermination squad and Vera Wohlauf, a sadistic concentration camp guard, are perhaps the easiest to understand in that they evidently lacked both a conscience and compassion. They sought out opportunities to satisfy their innate cruelty and could not imagine ever having to answer for their crimes.

More difficult to decipher are the female nurses and doctors who sought to justify their participation in sadistic medical experiments and the state-authorized euthanasia programme, a programme which the regime tried to keep secret from the population because it involved the legalized murder of German citizens. Nurse Irmgard Huber was just one of numerous 'Brown Sisters' who willingly participated in the 'mercy killing' of an estimated 15,000 people, including hundreds of German children, rationalizing her involvement by telling herself that she facilitated their humane extinction. Her colleague, Pauline Kneissler, exemplified the corrupted mentality of those complicit in the murder of 'useless eaters' by claiming that she had never mistreated a patient whom she had selected for death.

But how do you explain the wanton cruelty of Dr Herta Oberheuser, the Ravensbrück concentration camp physician, whose disregard for the suffering of her unwilling victims not only contravened the physician's oath but also basic human decency? Her distorted perception of what constituted ethical medical procedures and what any reasonable person would consider torture was examined at Nuremberg during the 'Doctors Trial', at which she and her co-defendants were charged with 'murders, brutalities, cruelties, tortures, atrocities and other inhuman acts'.

Others chose to deny the evidence in order to preserve their memory of a beloved parent or partner, even when that person had been convicted of war crimes. Brigitte Hoess, daughter of Auschwitz commandant Rudolf Hoess, appears to have been afflicted with the same syndrome as some of the wives of the SS men, such as Elfriede Suhren, who sought to justify their loyalty to their partners by constructing a false reality for themselves. And yet Rudolf Hoess had voluntarily made a full written confession on 16 March 1946 and again shortly before his execution, which his daughter and the Holocaust deniers predictably dismissed as having been torn out of him under torture.

Perhaps most baffling of all are the women who turned on their own kind, such as pretty Berliner Stella Goldschlag, who ensnared and betrayed her fellow Jews, motivated by what appears to have been self-hatred as much as self-preservation.

More typical perhaps was Marianne Gartner, who exemplified the 'ordinary' German. She was a simple middle-class girl who grew up during the Hitler years knowing nothing of life before the Third Reich and who recorded her impressions of life under the dictator with more insight than most of her generation.

Marianne's contemporaries in the *Bund Deutscher Mädel* (BDM), the female branch of the Hitler Youth, provide a very different perspective. Like Ilse Hirsch 'the female werewolf', many began with a childlike enthusiasm for a movement they believed would make Germany master of Europe and ended up fighting and dying for a man who had cynically betrayed them as well as the ideal they had misguidedly believed in. As one young convert remarked: 'We were the new youth; the old people just had to learn to think in the new way and it was our job to make them see the ideals of the new nationalized Germany.'

The degree of indoctrination to which they were subjected can be discerned in the uncritical account of Hildegard Trutz, a young fanatic who gave birth for Hitler as a member of the insidious Lebensborn SS breeding programme.

Their experiences were in stark contrast to those of Melita Maschmann, a former member of the BDM, who came to realize that she had been manipulated by the regime. She tried to make amends by publishing a 'confession' that opened a lot of eyes in post-war Germany to the silent crime that had been perpetrated on countless girls and young women of her generation – the betrayal of innocence.

CHAPTER ONE

Paula, Hitler's Sister

The diaries of Hitler's sister Paula support the generally accepted version of Hitler's early years, in which he suffered at the hands of a brutal and domineering father and was supported by a doting and indulgent mother.

However, her account of Hitler's 'extraordinary interest' in scholastic subjects is at odds with that of his teachers, who criticized his poor academic results. Her description of her young brother as 'cheerful' also conflicts with the many instances in which he struck her hard and repeatedly with his 'loose hand'.

Paula's diaries call into question Hitler's later account of the time when he had to live on the streets of Vienna, sleeping in doss-houses, because she reveals that he was in receipt of a modest but adequate pension at the time.

Her description of her brother as a man who was 'radiant with kindness' is perhaps the furthest from the truth, but this does not necessarily suggest that the contents of the diaries are untrue. It perhaps just means that as a loving sister Paula could not see the monster that her brother had become.

The notorious forged 'Hitler Diaries' hoax, perpetuated in the 1980s, has made historians naturally wary of anyone claiming to have unearthed handwritten journals by eminent Nazis and particularly by those who were close to Hitler. Thought to have been written by Adolf Hitler himself, the Hitler Diaries had in fact been forged by illustrator Konrad Kujau between 1981 and 1983. In 1983, they were bought by the German magazine *Stern* and publication rights were sold to, among others, the UK's *Sunday Times*. The hoax was uncovered when the diaries were belatedly subjected to a proper forensic examination, by which time a number of eminent academic reputations and editorial careers had been destroyed.

But the recently discovered diaries of Hitler's sister, Paula, have proved to be authentic, according to Dr Timothy Ryback, the head of Germany's Obersalzberg Institute of Contemporary History, and author Florian Beierl. Her journal records the often traumatic experiences of the Hitler children at the hands of their brutal, domineering father Alois and the effect that they had on Adolf, his older half-sister Angela and his half-brother, also called Alois.

Paula began the diary when she was eight and Adolf was fifteen. His volatile temper was already in evidence by then and he habitually lashed out at his little sister at the slightest provocation. She complained of being struck hard and repeatedly by his 'loose hand', then timorously found excuses to justify his abusive behaviour. She also described the beatings meted out by an enraged and often inebriated Alois Snr. and their mother's vain attempts to intervene.

More significantly, her account reveals that she was not the naive innocent that she later claimed to be, but was at one time engaged to Austrian physician Dr Erwin Jekelius, who was active in the Nazi euthanasia programme. He was accused of having gassed 4,000 of the mentally and physically disabled who were deemed by the Nazis to be 'unworthy of life'. Ironically, it was Adolf who prevented her from marrying Jekelius. On hearing that Jekelius was intending to ask for his sister's hand, the Führer had the physician arrested by the Gestapo on his arrival in Berlin and reassigned to the Russian front.

Early days of a dictator

The journal is not the only surviving record of Paula's early years with Hitler. On 5 June 1946, she was interviewed by American Intelligence and her testimony recorded in English. Paula was born in Hafeld (upper Austria) when her parents still owned a small farm, but as Alois, a retired customs official, was by then 58 years old and in poor health, he was forced to sell it. Of the four surviving children from her father's third marriage, she was fondest of Adolf, who had been christened Adolphus but was known in the family as Adi.

Paula maintained that her parents' marriage was a 'very happy one' despite their age difference – Alois was 23 years older than his wife – and the contrast in their temperaments. Their mother was docile and indulgent while her husband was strict and easily enraged. He was quick to find fault with his children who were 'very lively and difficult to train' though he 'spoiled' Paula, which must have angered Adolf even more and would have given him cause

> **PAULA WAS NO INNOCENT. SHE WAS AT ONE TIME ENGAGED TO AUSTRIAN PHYSICIAN DR ERWIN JEKELIUS, WHO WAS ACTIVE IN THE NAZI EUTHANASIA PROGRAMME**

to resent her. According to Paula, the children were the cause of the majority of arguments between the 'harsh' disciplinarian and the 'tender' mother. Adolf resisted his father's authority and provoked him at every opportunity, for which he suffered almost daily beatings.

> He was a scrubby little rogue, and all attempts of his father to thrash him for his rudeness and to cause him to love the profession of an official of the estate were in vain. How often on the other hand did my mother caress him and try to obtain with her kindness where the father could not succeed with harshness!

Her highly selective memory and description of her brother as 'cheerful' and possessing an 'extraordinary interest for history, geography, architecture, painting and music' is in stark contrast to his teachers' assessment, which criticized the boy's sullen, opinionated personality, insolent attitude and poor academic results. At home, Paula remembers being 'lectured' by her brother on history and politics, subjects on which he considered himself to be an authority. Brother and sister would 'quarrel frequently' and she submitted to his will very reluctantly. It 'spoiled' the atmosphere of the home, she recalled, and yet they remained fond of each other.

An embittered boy

Alois died in January 1903 from heart failure, to the relief of his eldest son, providing his widow with a decent pension, a portion of which she used to purchase a piano for her darling Adi. Paula recalls her brother 'sitting for hours' at the 'beautiful Heintzman grand', although he had only the most rudimentary understanding of music and no patience for learning the instrument. It was the idea of being an artist that appealed to the indolent adolescent. Adolf Hitler was a dreamer who lacked the self-discipline to study anything seriously and he became even more embittered as he grew older, when he realized he would never fulfil his artistic ambitions. But in the years following his father's death he indulged his passion for operas, particularly those written by Richard Wagner, whose mythical Ring cycle he saw 13 times in one year.

Four years later, on 21 December 1907, their mother died of cancer. Paula and Adolf nursed her during her protracted illness and Paula remembered that he proved to be a loving son; tender, considerate and eager to do whatever he could to make her final days tolerable.

With both parents gone, their mother's widow's pension was discontinued and Adolf was obliged to find work. An aunt made a final attempt to persuade him to seek a position in the civil service, but the 17-year-old was determined to pursue his artistic ambitions as either a water colourist or an architect.

He had abandoned his hopes of becoming a pianist after his only childhood friend, August Kubizek, had been accepted into the conservatoire in Vienna and in doing so had exposed Hitler's grand plans as nothing but the idle dreams of youth.

When Hitler was rejected by the Viennese Academy of Fine Arts that year, and again the following year, he blamed the selection committee whom he imagined had conspired to deny him his destiny, rather than admit the possibility that his work was simply not up to standard. In his largely fictitious biography and manifesto *Mein Kampf*, he described how he had suffered at the hands of the predominantly Jewish committee and how he was forced to live on the streets of Vienna selling his crude watercolours and sleeping in doss-houses. In fact, he was at the time living comparatively comfortably on a legacy of 900 Kroner per year (it would perhaps be worth £8,000 to £9,000 [some $12,000] in 2018), as revealed by the family accounts which were discovered at the same time as Paula's journal.

Living in her brother's shadow

Paula lost contact with her brother during this time, only meeting him again in 1921, 13 years later, after she too had moved to Vienna. He had not lost his appetite for self-aggrandizement, informing her that he had had 'wonderful adventures' during the 1914–18 war and raving about the bond of 'comradeship' he had enjoyed. The truth was that he was despised by his comrades, who considered him 'intolerable' because he never laughed unless it was at the misfortune of others and named him the 'White Crow' because he was radically different from everyone else. Despite demonstrating his bravery under fire, he was not promoted because his superiors believed that the men would not follow him.

By the time of their brief reunion, Hitler had become leader of the nascent NSDAP and was living in Munich. The reason for his temporary return to Vienna is unknown, but it enabled the pair to renew their friendship and allowed Paula to see that her brother had not died in the trenches as she had assumed. Evidently, he had not thought to contact her on his return, contradicting her idealized image of him as a considerate older sibling. She then returned to her job as a secretary 'in an insignificant office', while he went back to Munich where he shared a house with his half-sister, Angela.

While Hitler's star was then in the ascendant, Paula's life was made more difficult by his increasing notoriety. She was dismissed from her job as the result of her family connection with a political agitator and felt it necessary to change her surname to Wolf, which oddly enough was the nickname Hitler adopted.

When he was made aware of Paula's situation he immediately offered to pay her a regular income of 250 marks a month, rising to 500, with an annual Christmas 'bonus' of 3,000 marks.

She claimed never to have been a member of the Nazi Party, but said that she would have joined had her brother asked her to. Predictably, she also maintained that she had not known of the crimes committed by his regime, nor of the existence of the concentration camps, a statement which her interrogator noted was 'unworthy of belief'. He also dismissed her assertion that she had been ignorant of her brother's threat to 'destroy the Jews in Europe' as these policies had been widely broadcast and publicized in the German and Austrian press and were common knowledge. Such 'tactics' were all too familiar to the Allies, who were already engaged in the denazification process. Paula's assertion that her brother was 'radiant with kindness' contrasted with the facts of his brutality and the merciless cruelty meted out to his enemies, combatants and civilians alike. Because of her feigned ignorance and guileless appearance, her interrogators concluded that Paula was a lonely and 'guiltless woman'. As with the surviving members of the Hitler family, she did not profit from her brother's influence, privilege and power and with the destruction of the Nazi state she and her kin returned to the peasant roots from which their most notorious relative had risen.

CHAPTER TWO

Hitler and the Braun Sisters

Eva Braun first met Hitler in 1929, when she was 17 years old and working for Heinrich Hoffmann, his personal photographer. At the time, Hitler was embroiled in a relationship with his half-niece Geli Raubal. Two years later, after Geli's death, he began to see more of Eva.

It is through the eyes of Eva's sister, Gretl, that we are able to see Eva and learn more about her relationship with Hitler.

His affair with Geli Raubal has been described by some sources as 'unnatural', but from what she observed Gretl insisted that he enjoyed normal sexual relations with Eva.

Some have written that Eva Braun was a token mistress, a ploy to hide Hitler's latent homosexual tendencies or perhaps even his impotence, but Gretl was convinced that 'he loved Eva' and that she adored him. Public displays of affection between Hitler and Eva were limited, but it may have been politically expedient for Hitler to appear to be a celibate who was 'married to Germany'. Whatever the case, Eva's relationship with Hitler was kept secret as far as was possible, with the press referring to her merely as his 'favourite'.

A photograph shows two young women smiling at the camera. They wear identical flower-patterned dresses with short puff sleeves and buttons down the centre, from the high, tight collar to the waist. They have on the same high-heeled shoes and they even wear their hair in the same style – plaited in a flat bun on top of their heads like a beret. Both of them are of the same height and slim build. It is clear they are sisters.

The picture has been taken outside in the bright spring or summer sun in what appears to be the countryside, possibly the mountains, with a white-walled, two-storey villa in the background – a typical Alpine building. If it was not for the figure seen in the open doorway in the middle distance one would assume this was a casual holiday snap taken in the late 1920s or early 1930s in Austria or Germany.

The figure is that of a man in uniform, as far as one can tell, with his jacket open, presumably keeping a watchful eye on the two young women and the unidentified photographer. His presence, even in such a seemingly informal setting, is revealing. Both women, it would seem, are under constant scrutiny. The girl on the right because she is the younger sister of Eva Braun, mistress of Adolf Hitler, at whose Alpine retreat this photo was taken.

Gretl Braun is certainly the more conventionally pretty of the two. Eva has the fuller face of a rosy-cheeked Bavarian 'milkmaid' and is prone to grinning inanely at the camera when filmed performing her daily exercises or picking flowers, while Gretl looks seriously into the lens, her thoughts kept to herself.

Gretl gave few interviews after the war. After all, her sister Eva had committed suicide in the Berlin bunker, with her new husband, Adolf Hitler, by her side. The longest was given to Hitler biographer John Toland in the small country town of Steingaden in Upper Bavaria over two days in January 1974. From Toland's unpublished notes in the archive of the Library of Congress in Washington, it is possible to elicit more details regarding the nature of the relationship between Hitler and Eva as well as an impression of her more reticent sister.

Developing relationship

Gretl recalled the first time she saw Hitler. It was in an Italian restaurant in Munich called the Osteria Bavaria, which was the future Führer's favourite place to eat and where he met his associates. Gretl had gone there to buy wine and bread rolls. Eva was not present, so it was Hitler's photographer Heinrich Hoffmann who introduced them. Gretl was only 16 at the time, and so Hitler had no need to acknowledge her, but she recalled that he was 'proper', 'friendly and polite' after he was informed she was Eva's sister.

> Hitler looked at me and said: 'I see the resemblance.' That really was all. He smiled, bowed a little bit. He did not kiss my hand ... he didn't make this overwhelming impression on me. The men he was sitting with were all a little rough-looking, it was intimidating.

At this time, Hitler was embroiled in an intense and, by all accounts, unnatural relationship with his half-niece Geli Raubal, who would later shoot herself. It was believed that Geli committed suicide because she could not cope with her domineering uncle's 'perverse' sexual demands nor his pathological jealousy, which forbade her to have relationships with other men, romantic or otherwise. According to Gretl, it was Geli's suicide on 18 September 1931 which prompted Hitler to become closer to Eva. It was not that he could confide in such a young girl – Eva was then just 19 years old – but he clearly craved the attention

> **HITLER VALUED EVA TREMENDOUSLY BECAUSE HE KNEW HE COULD BE SURE SHE WOULD KEEP THEIR RELATIONSHIP TO HERSELF**

of women – both young girls and maternal figures such as his patron Winifred Wagner – and he was gratified by her obvious concern for his well-being, though he hated to be 'fussed over'.

It flattered the 42-year-old to be surrounded by pretty young girls and to be the centre of attention and it fed into his vanity, but Eva also served to assuage his abnormal grief for his niece, to whom he had built a shrine. He forbade anyone from entering Geli's room, which he preserved just as it had been on the day she died.

Eva's attentiveness distracted him and, according to Gretl, Hitler 'valued her tremendously' because he knew he could be sure she would keep their relationship to herself. This was crucial as he feared that an affair – especially one involving a young girl – would fatally damage his political career, which was already severely weakened by the scandal of Geli's apparent suicide. Hitler's enemies and political rivals (some of whom were within his own party) stoked the rumours that she had been murdered and there is sufficient evidence to support this claim, as I wrote in *Nazi Women*. Eva's discretion was 'a big determining factor in Hitler settling down with her', according to her sister, who became aware of their relationship when Eva's absences became more frequent and prolonged.

Sometimes she didn't come home until long after midnight. She got her own private telephone line and would hide under her covers when she spoke to this mysterious man … We shared a bedroom, so I knew of her comings and goings.

But the matter was kept secret from their parents whom Eva would casually lie to, telling them that she was working late at Hoffmann's photographic studio. They suspected nothing and had no reason to distrust their middle daughter, who was circumspect and not the type to boast of an 'affair', if that was how it could be described. Eva was also acutely aware that a romantic liaison with an older man was frowned upon in German society at that time and would have ruined her reputation.

Attention-seeking ploy?

In the early days of their relationship Hitler was away from Munich for much of the time and their affair had to be conducted by telephone, using a long-distance line installed in the house of a wealthier friend, Herta Ostermeyer.

The nature of their relationship has been the subject of much fevered speculation over the years, but Gretl is adamant that it was a normal physical one. Eva never spoke of it in those terms, but

she started hiding things in our room. Personal garments, contraceptives, letters, things that a romantic young girl does during her first love affair. She was having an affair, even I knew that and I was only 16 or 17 myself.

Hitler's public displays of affection were limited to hand-holding and tracing a circle distractedly around her face with his finger. 'As for kissing, embracing, carrying on together,' said Gretl, nothing of that nature was seen. 'Never.'

Before he became Chancellor, Hitler would take Eva to the opera, the cinema and to dinner, but always in the company of his entourage. It was only at the end of the evening that he would order his driver to take them to his private apartment so that they could be alone.

But still Eva was not content with the degree of attention he was paying her and in November 1932 she attempted suicide for the first time, although Gretl believed it was not a serious attempt. Eva was found by their eldest sister Ilse, bleeding from a self-inflicted bullet wound. Eva's friend, Marion Schönmann, who claimed to have been in the apartment at the time, was convinced it had been staged to get Hitler's attention. By the time he arrived, clutching flowers and a 'get well' card, the patient had been worked on by Erna Hoffmann, who utilized her make-up skills to blanch Eva's pallid complexion and give her the appearance of a 'distressed' suicide.

Second suicide attempt

After Hitler became Chancellor on 30 January 1933, Eva felt no need to justify her frequent absences from home. She told her parents that she was now accompanying her boss, Heinrich Hoffmann, 'on the road' with his one and only client, Adolf Hitler, and that she would stay overnight on a more regular basis without offering an explanation. Although she continued to work at the photographer's shop, Eva was now spending more time at the Berghof, Hitler's private residence near Berchtesgaden, and at his Munich apartment. Her increasing absences gave Gretl the opportunity to take her place at the photographer's shop and to see Hitler on a more regular and informal basis.

Gretl formed the impression that he was 'a normal, nice, friendly man ... very charming, very fatherly'. She credited him with 'a funny sense of humour ... He was not the monster shown today on TV or in magazines. Not in the slightest.' But of course, Gretl never saw him in his official capacity surrounded by his acolytes – those entrusted with carrying out his edicts and orders. She claimed that he never flirted with her as 'he would have considered that rude and indelicate because I was Eva's sister'. But he was not so circumspect with other women.

Eva did not take such harmless dalliances lightly and her romantic schoolgirl fantasy did not allow for rivals. The longer his absences became (for he never invited her to accompany him) the more intense her dissatisfaction grew until on 28 May 1935 she made a second melodramatic suicide attempt. This time she took an overdose of Veronal (the first commercially available barbiturate, which was commonly used as a sleeping draught) but not until she was sure to be interrupted. Her stomach was pumped and by the time she recovered Hitler was at her bedside, promising to rent an apartment of her own on Widenmayerstrasse, which she would share with Gretl. There the pair could threw parties and 'do the things young girls like to do when away from their parents' gaze'. But the illicit thrill of being the Führer's mistress was blighted by the knowledge that Eva's parents disapproved of her 'shameful' lifestyle. As Gretl explained:

> My father would never have come to visit. He detested Eva's choice in a man and the fact Hitler had set her up in an apartment. To him it was deeply humiliating that she was living with a man at his own whim at an apartment he was paying for.

Hitler the attentive lover

According to Gretl, who made herself scarce when Hitler arrived, his scheduled visits were infrequent and restricted to the evening when it was dark. He was always accompanied by an SS guard, whose car would be parked outside, a sign for Gretl to stay away until Eva was alone. In the five months that the sisters lived there, Hitler visited no more than four or five times. He rarely stayed more than a few hours and never spent the night. Hitler's obsession with privacy finally prompted him to relinquish the flat and buy Eva a modest house in Wasserburger Strasse so that she could play hausfrau to the man she called 'the greatest in Germany and the whole world'.

Although Hitler was officially a millionaire from the royalties accruing from *Mein Kampf* and the nominal percentage he earned from the sales of postage stamps bearing his image, he never paid for anything he didn't have to. Hoffmann was required to purchase the house and furniture and pay all of the bills from the fortune he had made selling photographs of the Führer.

Hitler was uncharacteristically credulous and indulgent when it came to Eva's 'playacting', the term Hoffmann used in private when referring to her fake suicide attempts. But he had been deeply upset by Geli's death – and perhaps also at the thought that he had precipitated it – and consequently he dreaded the thought that his plans could be disrupted by another traumatic episode. Women, he once thoughtlessly remarked in Eva's presence, were 'stupid' but also

> **ALTHOUGH HITLER WAS A MILLIONAIRE, HE NEVER PAID FOR ANYTHING HE DIDN'T HAVE TO. HOFFMANN WAS REQUIRED TO BUY THE HOUSE AND PAY ALL THE BILLS**

unpredictable. Humouring his mistress may have been a matter of simple expediency, therefore, because he could not afford another scandal even after his assumption of the Chancellorship. He needed to be seen as the 'strong man' Germany had been seeking, someone who could restore its pride after the crushing defeat of 1914–18; a father figure to replace the Kaiser, who had been forced to abdicate in November 1918, leaving the nation leaderless and at the mercy of rival political factions on the far left and extreme right. He was aware that the plans of 'great men' could be undermined by a weakness for women. Even so, he was not unaffected by his disagreements with Eva.

As Gretl recalled:

> I have also seen Hitler upset when they had been having words. He was not immune from being bothered or upset by their relationship. He was an emotional man; he had tremendous highs and he could get low as well, I've seen it.

He was not a man who showed his feelings other than when indulging in his infamous rages, which were often staged for effect, to intimidate an adversary, but Gretl suspected that in private he might be different with Eva. He knew how to placate and charm her, as he did with his numerous female admirers. But she described him as the 'most private individual' she had ever seen, a 'very secretive' person.

> I am convinced that he loved Eva and there is absolutely no question of her complete adoration of him. He was away all the time because his position demanded it. She couldn't travel with him because their relationship was supposed to be secret.

HITLER WAS NOT A MAN WHO SHOWED HIS FEELINGS OTHER THAN INDULGING IN HIS INFAMOUS RAGES WHICH WERE OFTEN ONLY FOR EFFECT

'Like a married couple'

For her part, Eva relished her role as the Führer's secret mistress, but it frustrated her to be left behind when he spent months away from her. 'She was inconsolable without him; that was a never-changing refrain.'

When they were apart, she would write him lengthy letters and cards, spending an hour or more every day composing them in her neat schoolgirl hand. They were sent via a trusted courier, such as the pilot Baur, Henriette Hoffmann, the photographer's daughter, or Hitler's adjutant, Brückner. Hitler's replies were brief, but she treasured them none the less and kept them in a safe at the Berghof. In one of her last phone calls to Gretl in May 1945, Eva begged her sister to bury them. By this time their letters were in the 'hundreds'. On Hitler's return he would console her by indulging their shared fantasy of living a simple bourgeois life in his motherland of Austria.

> Beginning around 1940, he openly told Eva that when the war was won, they would build a beautiful house in Linz, overlooking the Pöstlingberg. I think he even had blueprints for the proposed house. He said they would be married. He even mentioned this to me, saying he hoped I would visit them.

Gretl told Toland that Hitler and her sister lived together 'like a married couple' and that he teased her by deliberately wearing ill-fitting and mismatched clothes that he knew would infuriate the fashion-conscious girl and by telling her that she was overweight and needed to go on a diet. They were intimate, said Gretl, but after the war started Hitler aged rapidly – a combination of the military reversals and the cocktail of drugs he was by then dependent upon were taking their toll on his mental and physical health. He became more distant as the war dragged on and, when he reached 53, in 1942, he even attempted to persuade Eva that she should leave him because he was 'too old for her', something she tearfully confided to both her younger sister and Hitler's armaments minister, Albert Speer. At this point, Gretl heard Hitler say that he could only trust two things: his dog Blondi and his mistress Eva Braun.

Brief marriage

Even as late as the first months of 1945, with the Russians encircling Berlin, Gretl and Eva shared the hope that a 'miracle' might still save them and that the Russians would retreat. But as hope faded Eva prepared for her last act of devotion to the dictator. Thirty-six hours before they committed suicide in the claustrophobic cell that served as Hitler's private study, she took the oath to stand by his side to the end in a brief civil marriage ceremony. Then as the guests partied in a bizarre atmosphere of strained cheerfulness she sent a final message to her elder sister Ilse, urging her to burn her dressmaker's bills because she did not want to be remembered as a vacuous fashion-obsessed shopaholic.

Gretl heard of her sister's death in May, through a wireless broadcast announcing the fact that she had killed herself alongside her Führer in the bunker.

'I was preparing for her death, but I didn't assume when she went to be with him that she would perish there.'

Predictably, Gretl insists that neither she nor Eva 'knew anything that was going on. Hitler didn't discuss politics or military matters with Eva. Not once.'

When asked how she could be sure that he did not discuss anything of that nature with her sister, Gretl answered:

Because she told me. She was always complaining later on, 'I know nothing that's going on'. They talked about other things: dogs, movies, music, Munich gossip, who was going with who, who was cheating on their spouses, who was drinking too much or trying to quit. All sorts of local things like that. Hitler had a very strong adolescent side to him, emotionally he was like a boy in certain things, like film stars and gossip.

I was Eva Braun's cousin

Gertrude Weisker was 20 years old in the summer of 1944 when she was invited to Berchtesgaden to keep her 32-year-old cousin Eva Braun company at the Berghof. It was to be the last summer of Eva's life. Travel was restricted due to the bombing, but as Gertrude's grandparents were in Munich she thought her father would agree to let her go. He forbade her but she went anyway. As with many Germans, she saw herself as a victim and insensitively and offensively compared the situation of ordinary citizens in the Reich to a 'concentration camp' when she was interviewed 50 years later by journalist Linda Grant at her home near Heidelberg.

Although the nature of Braun's relationship with Hitler was a secret, her existence was public knowledge and the press explained her presence by saying that she was the Führer's 'favourite'. Gertrude was in awe of her cousin.

> She was very sporty, and to me she was very beautiful ... but she was, in my eyes, always trying to do something, to be active. I don't know why. There was a special emptiness in her and she was trying to fill it by sport, by swimming. Things which don't matter. She always changed dresses, five times, seven times a day ... Sometimes she was a Bavarian girl, sometimes she was a lady, and maybe that was to fill her emptiness. There was no one to adore her.

A typical teenager, Gertrude was unimpressed by her surroundings and soon became bored.

To relieve the tedium, she went through the rooms until she came upon a radio and then tuned into the BBC, a treasonable act which carried the death penalty. Ignoring the risk, she made copious notes and gave her cousin a daily report detailing the Allied advance, which had a sobering effect on Eva.

'Eva listened carefully and in time she completely changed … I think she prepared herself very carefully for her death.'

By Christmas Munich was under heavy bombardment and one night, while the cousins huddled together in the shelter, Eva opened a suitcase full of jewellery and offered it to her young companion with the words: 'I don't need this any more.'

Gertrude left Munich shortly after hearing that her father was ill. Had she stayed, she believes Eva might have remained at the Berghof and not died by Hitler's side in Berlin.

Gertrude was adamant that neither she nor Eva were Nazis. And yet she kept a photograph of Hitler in the family album while maintaining strict silence regarding her kinship to his mistress who, at the very end, became his wife. Gertrude's future husband stipulated when they married that she was not to speak of Eva Braun until a decade after his death, not even to their own children – especially not to them!

More bizarre is the fact that Gertrude became a chat show celebrity after a novel was published in which she played a central role, albeit under a pseudonym, expressing thoughts and insights regarding Eva's relationship with Hitler which bore no relation to her own ideas.

In Linda Grant's words, the novel *Eva's Cousin* by Sibylle Knauss has spun a 'web of false memory' around Gertrude, whose fictitious alter ego has given the old woman a new life and made sense of her old one. As for Eva Braun, Knauss concluded that her role was to convince Hitler that he was a human being capable of feelings which he probably did not possess.

CHAPTER THREE

Hitler's Female Admirers

It certainly can't have been Hitler's looks that attracted his female followers – he was almost the antithesis of the Nazi Party's ideal blond-haired Aryan. Yet 'hysterical' young women even scooped up the stones on which he had walked as souvenirs.

Perhaps inspired by his air of self-belief, many women saw Hitler as the new messiah, someone who would not only transform the fortunes of a humiliated and impoverished Germany but who was also concerned about the welfare of each and every one of them. The dictator received thousands of letters from his female admirers, some quite explicit, not to mention gifts of all kinds.

But the semblance of altruism and a promised economic miracle could not account for all of the adulation. Maybe it was Hitler's portraying himself as an unobtainable celibate who was only in love with Germany that made him attractive? Or was it the way in which he seemed to be able to reach into the very soul of each one of his listeners?

In the words of Henry Kissinger, the answer might just be that 'power is the ultimate aphrodisiac'. The flow of letters slowed down to a dribble and then almost ceased when Hitler's fortunes waned.

Contrary to popular myth, Hitler did not owe his electoral successes to female voters. In the presidential election of March 1932, when the Nazis secured their largest share of the vote, only a quarter of the women who went to the polling stations backed Hitler, whereas twice that number voted for Hindenburg. In the previous September, more women had cast their vote for the conservative nationalist parties than for the NSDAP, who secured three million votes from their female followers, half as many as they accumulated from their male supporters.

But the fact remains that Hitler won over a substantial proportion of women whose approval and support was crucial in the early 1930s. He had tens of thousands of women fawning and weeping over him like starry-eyed schoolgirls whenever he made a public appearance and numerous wealthy female patrons funding the Party and facilitating meetings with influential financiers and industrialists. Their endorsement helped to assuage the anxieties of those who felt compelled to vote for the Nazis because they seemed to be the only alternative to communism or chaos.

Being surrounded by adoring, attractive young women and socialites softened Hitler's image. They gave him an aura of respectability and made him appear less threatening than in the 1920s, when he presented himself as a beer-hall agitator in Bavarian lederhosen and carrying a riding crop.

Had the women of Germany and Austria been less eager to believe in their false messiah, had they been less ingenuous and more discerning, history might have taken a very different course. But they were swept up in the wave of euphoria that surged through Germany and few had the strength to resist the irrational collective will.

BEING SURROUNDED BY ADORING, ATTRACTIVE WOMEN AND SOCIALITES SOFTENED HITLER'S IMAGE AND MADE HIM APPEAR LESS THREATENING

It was self-belief, not physical attraction or charisma, that captivated Hitler's audiences and convinced them that anything was possible. Any individual who possesses this trait and who knows intuitively how to exploit the fears of the masses and pander to their prejudices, as Hitler did, can manipulate them and they will worship him in spite of his flaws. The women of Germany convinced themselves that the Führer was a good God-fearing Catholic who was solid and sincere in his stated desires to address their concerns and was a safe pair of hands in which to entrust their future and that of their families.

Mountains of fan mail

Traudl Junge, the youngest of Hitler's private secretaries, recalled the 'hysterical' young women who made special pilgrimages to the Berghof, Hitler's mountain retreat, to collect the stones that he walked on during his morning strolls. Some even scooped up soil from the footpath and bottled it as if it was a sacred relic.

The garden fence too was stripped, a target of compulsive souvenir-hunters. Even tiles that had only just been delivered and were yet to be fitted in the Führer's bathroom were stolen by 'a few very overexcited women' and put on display in their living room cabinets for the veneration of visitors.

This adulation generated mountains of fan mail which poured into Hitler's adjutancy at the rate of several hundred letters per day, requiring the attention of his secretaries and clerical staff. More than a thousand of these private letters were retrieved after the war by Wilhelm K. Eucker, a former member of the German resistance who had fled to France and subsequently joined the OSS (a forerunner of the CIA). Eucker found them lying scattered on the floor of the Reich Chancellery in the spring of 1946 and assumed that the Russians had not considered them worth saving. It is true that the Soviets had already seized all the documents they thought worth preserving, among which was a large cache of private correspondence which remained stored unseen and undisturbed in the Soviet military archives in Moscow. More documents were deposited in the German Bundesarchiv and in the Library of Congress, which had acquired its own collection of 'Hitler papers' in 1948.

> **FAN MAIL POURED INTO HITLER'S ADJUTANCY AT THE RATE OF SEVERAL HUNDRED LETTERS PER DAY, REQUIRING THE ATTENTION OF HIS SECRETARIES**

A random selection of extracts from these private letters gives a fair impression of the intensity of emotions the dictator aroused in his female admirers; from the sincere, the sad and the desperate to the outright insane. More importantly, they give a sense of the mindset of these women, whose ages ranged from pre-teen to elderly.

Gifts and offers of love

One of the first female admirers to write to Hitler in the early years was 35-year-old activist Elsbeth Zander, who had founded the *Deutscher Frauenorden* (German Women's Order) in 1923, the year of the failed Munich putsch. By 1928 her organization would be affiliated with the NSDAP and would boast 4,000 members. In May 1925 Zander wrote to ask if Hitler would consider travelling outside Bavaria and if so would he address her members in Magdeburg and Berlin, who were anxious to hear him in person, despite the fact that her organization campaigned for the exclusion of women from public life. She urged him to take part in the Germany Day celebrations in Breslau too and stressed that 'people will only see it as a complete success if you do so'.

Rudolf Hess, Hitler's private secretary, replied, agreeing to a visit, but stated that Hitler would only speak to 'a small group of important people', who would have to be wealthy contributors to the Party coffers. (Hitler did not employ the first of several female secretaries until 1929.)

Zander would be marginalized by the Party in 1931 amid accusations of mismanagement and corruption and her role assumed by the formidable Gertrud Scholtz-Klink, 'the female Führer', who led the rival National Socialist Women's League from October that year.

There were numerous letters from men too, of course, but they were in the minority and most of these dated from the early years, when the Party membership was predominantly male, almost exclusively so. Their devotion to the former Austrian corporal expressed what has been called a 'crisis of masculinity' following the defeat of 1918. And though Germany remained a devoutly religious society on the whole, particularly in the Catholic south and in Austria, there was also a spiritual malaise after the losses of the Great War, when Hitler was seen by many as the answer to their prayers. For this reason, the letters contain countless religious allusions and references to Hitler using the reverential He and Him, recasting him as their God or saviour.

There were pleas for clemency on behalf of friends and family languishing in concentration camps and a small number of letters registering disapproval of the regime, at a time when doing so would not invite a visit from the Gestapo. The vast majority of letters, however, were rapturous expressions of appreciation for the restoration of their pride and the promise of 'work and bread' which had saved so many families from impoverishment and some from starvation.

Letters from women took a somewhat different tack. There were earnest and effusive notes accompanying socks, silk handkerchiefs, carpets, home-made cakes and marriage contracts, the latter with a space left blank for the Führer to sign if he accepted their proposal.

Countless women offered themselves enthusiastically and without commitment, eager to gratify their own sexual longing and imagining that Hitler would appreciate their ardent sacrifice. There were donations for Hitler to distribute to worthy causes, including a substantial 8,000-mark inheritance from one Margarthe Rathmann in Potsdam, near Berlin. And there were poems; reams and reams of embarrassingly trite and poorly executed verse expressing undying love and devotion.

The handkerchiefs were returned by Hess, now Deputy Führer, with a curt and dismissive note admonishing the sender for embroidering them with the image of the Führer without having first obtained his permission. Hess was not the most tactful of assistants, but he took every opportunity to plug his chief's book, informing numerous correspondents that they would find the answer to their questions in the pages of *Mein Kampf*. He had assisted Hitler with writing it while they were both languishing in Landsberg prison.

Gaining female support

Five years before the infamous Nuremberg Laws deprived German Jews of their citizenship and basic human rights, the Nazis were a minority presence in the Reichstag and so were unable to implement their malicious racial policies.

Their newly won supporters, however, were free to express their extreme views. In February 1930, a Peenemünde hausfrau, Frau von Ponief, wrote to Hitler calling for a boycott of Jewish businesses, prompting Hess to reply that the Party had every intention of doing so, but that it would be illegal for them to campaign for one now. Despite the Party's increasing popularity and vast membership, the political situation was still highly volatile. Hitler had his eyes on the September election, which would see him criss-crossing the country by aeroplane to make hundreds of speeches, as a result of which the National Socialist share of the vote would rise to 18.3 per cent (6,371,000 votes), giving them 107 seats in the Reichstag and making them the second-largest party in the German parliament.

The Nazis had benefited from the economic uncertainty and political instability following the Wall Street Crash of 1929, just as they had capitalized on the hyperinflation which had plagued Germany early in that decade. The Crash reawakened fears of the hourly price increases which had seen employees insist on their wages each lunchtime to be sure of being able to afford to buy food before the prices doubled or tripled by closing time. It also raised the spectre of endemic unemployment, which Hitler had promised to counter with an extensive programme of public works that would put every able-bodied man back to work.

His vision for a new Germany inspired thousands who had no previous interest in politics to find their voice and to discover that their illogical and absurd retrogressive beliefs were shared by their new leaders.

In December 1930 32-year-old Elsa Walter, an unmarried woman from Karlsruhe, wrote to Hitler enclosing an 80-page clothbound handwritten book entitled *The German Woman*, in which she detailed her reasons for having joined the Party the previous month, reasons which she believed were shared by many women.

The Nazi leadership would have been reassured to read Elsa Walter's thesis, in which she pleaded the case for German women to abandon their careers and remain at home to be 'the soul of the house' and the nation. The 'modern athletic girl', she wrote, should not be the model for German women, because their 'unhealthy ambition' to find employment outside the home and to expect equal rights would surely prove detrimental to the 'natural' relationship of the sexes. Men, she argued, would be in danger of being made redundant in every respect if the 'women and girls of today' exercised their right to prove that they were of equal intelligence. There was already a forgotten army of unemployed men, many of them veterans of the 1914–18 war, whose jobs had been appropriated by young ambitious 'career girls'. The 'masculinization' of these girls was 'unnatural', in her opinion, and was due partly to the emphasis placed on higher education.

Gullibility

The gullibility and willingness of these women to believe what they had been told is particularly disturbing. Towards the end of her ponderous, rambling monologue Fraülein Walter confesses that she was profoundly impressed by the explanation Hitler had given for the Party's adoption of the swastika as its symbol. He had apparently claimed that the hooked cross had been chosen because the National Socialists 'were not yet worthy of bearing the Christian cross'.

This from the man who would proclaim Christianity to be a dead religion and whose avowed intention was to replace the cross with the swastika, the Bible with *Mein Kampf* and Jesus with himself. He would be represented in neo-pagan ceremonies to mark every significant stage of the nation's life – birth, marriage and even death.

Fräulein Walter evidently had an 'issue' with natural and intimate relationships between the sexes and sought an endorsement of her peculiar fixations in Party policy, specifically those relating to contraception and those aspects of 'marriage and birth' about which the Social Democrats were lecturing in terms 'which cause a decent woman to blush with embarrassment'.

HITLER HAD DEVOTED TEN PAGES OF HIS MANIFESTO TO THE SCOURGE OF VENEREAL DISEASE, A SUBJECT IN WHICH HE CONSIDERED HIMSELF AN EXPERT

Had the leader of any other political party received such a lengthy and effusive letter, they would doubtless have tossed it into the wastepaper basket, but then Fräulein Walter and the scores of similarly minded women who wrote such letters to Hitler were addressing the man who had devoted ten pages of his political manifesto to the scourge of venereal disease, a subject in which he considered himself an expert.

After Hitler's appointment to the Chancellorship on 30 January 1933, his office was inundated with letters from young women asking for clerical positions in the new government. Some were veiled begging letters from girls with starving siblings, whose parents had no prospects for employment, or so they claimed. Others simply wanted a handout and assumed that if they expressed support for the leadership in flattering terms they would be suitably rewarded.

That Christmas, a nun wrote requesting a complimentary copy of *Mein Kampf*, because she professed to be too poor to buy one. She claimed to have been divinely inspired to write directly to the author so that she could use it to 'educate the big girls entrusted to me in a very national way'. In return, she would pray daily for 'rich blessings on the successful realization of your difficult but uniquely beautiful task'.

Many more were sincere and heartfelt expressions of gratitude from mothers who felt that they and their children were valued as citizens of the Reich. In appreciation, they enclosed photographs of their offspring to prove that they were practising what Hitler preached, assuming that these would bring a smile to the Führer's face and make his burdensome duties easier to bear. One proud mother boasted that her infant son dutifully raised his arm in the Hitler salute every time he heard the words of the Horst Wessel song (the 'Horst Wessel Lied', the Nazi Party anthem) while another wrote that her ten-month-old daughter did the same when shown a photo of her Führer. If Hitler was told about this, his reaction was not recorded.

Female pet owners who presumably did not have any family photos sent in embroidered pictures of their cats and dogs.

Asking the Reich for assistance

The women's motherly concern for Hitler's health revealed itself in the boxes of lozenges and other home-made remedies that followed the announcement that Hitler had given himself a sore throat after a particularly strident rant on the radio. This outpouring of misguided affection for their Führer was frequently tainted by a bitter and deep-seated suspicion of those who did not share their convictions, specifically the Jews, a prejudice which Hitler exploited for his own ends. It was rooted in malicious urban myths and fairy tales ingrained in the anti-Semitic psyche of the bigoted and uneducated peasant classes, but it was certainly not confined to them.

In May 1933, 13-year-old Annelene K. wrote urging 'Onkel Adolf' to intervene on behalf of the German-speaking population of Heydekrug, in what is now Lithuania. They were being persecuted, she said, for practising their new religion – National Socialism – by the 'Szameites', the Lithuanians who spoke a degraded form of German, and also by the Jews. They were expressly forbidden to wear or display the swastika and to greet each other with the customary Nazi salute, or say 'Heil Hitler' in public. She blamed the Jews not only for taking the bread from their mouths but also for 'sacrificing Christians at Easter time', a morbid fantasy of the kind that was still rife in early twentieth century Europe. And again, she cited Horst Wessel as a heroic symbol of defiance and inspiration – another Nazi myth so many had swallowed in blind faith. The 22-year-old Wessel was a pimp who had been killed in a fight with a Communist over a prostitute in January 1930. He was subsequently elevated to political martyrdom by the Nazis, who were masters at rewriting history to serve their own ends. But with the Party already controlling the major newspapers at that time, there was little chance of the truth being made public.

Annelene signed off as 'your little 13¾-year-old niece'. But even that affectation failed to elicit a reply. She was not the only young woman to think of Hitler as one of the family. In April 1934, farmer's daughter Susanne Hesse wrote from Thuringia to ask the Führer to intervene in the matter of her unrequited love for a baron. She also asked Hitler not to make anything 'public', which reveals her limited grip on reality, a common phenomenon among his besotted admirers.

> **ANNELENE SIGNED OFF AS 'YOUR LITTLE 13¾-YEAR-OLD NIECE'. SHE WAS NOT THE ONLY YOUNG WOMAN TO THINK OF HITLER AS ONE OF THE FAMILY**

But among the countless 'crank' letters entreating Hitler to intervene in trivial or personal matters were a number begging the Führer to intercede in serious matters. These were invariably dealt with by Hitler's chief adjutant, Wilhelm Brückner, with typical Prussian efficiency.

One such case was that of Frau Elsa Menzel whose husband, Colonel Paul Menzel of the SA, had been arrested by the Prussian military police on charges of embezzling Party funds. Brückner wrote to the Gestapo instructing them to check if Colonel Menzel had been falsely accused, as his wife had insisted, and in due course the colonel was released.

Writing to the Reich Chancellery to protest about an injustice was, however, an extremely risky enterprise. In the winter of 1934 more than a thousand people were sent to concentration camps after their letters protesting the persecution of Jehovah's Witnesses were forwarded to the Gestapo for 'further processing'.

Deification

To circumvent the bureaucracy of the Reich Chancellery and ensure more chance of success some correspondents wrote to Hitler's half-sister Angela Raubal, who acted as his housekeeper at the Berghof in Obersalzberg. After she married a Dresden professor, Hitler's mistress, Eva Braun, took over as hostess. Few members of the public knew of her existence and so direct access to the Führer became almost impossible thereafter.

Many correspondents, however, only wanted to express their devotion and appreciation, expecting nothing in return save perhaps an autographed photo which they promised to frame and hang in a prominent place in their humble homes. Such veneration for a national leader or politician would be inconceivable today, but it satisfied an almost religious yearning, so much so that even Hitler's mother was honoured on Mother's Day with letters giving thanks for the blessing she had bestowed on the nation by giving birth to 'the greatest of all architects'.

This idolatry moved some to deify him. A letter signed 'Baroness Else Hagen von Kilvein' concluded with the words: 'I have no God but you and no Gospel but your teaching.' The 'Baroness' was not alone in her praise. Many women addressed their beloved leader in similar terms and shared her sentiments.

The credulity and trust expressed by some of the women who wrote to Hitler in the wake of the *Anschluss*, the annexation of Austria, in March 1938 is breath-taking. Oblivious to the fact that Vienna had seen Jew-baiting and persecution on a scale that shocked some of the Germans, Julie Oesterle, an elderly woman from Bregenz, wrote to the Führer to congratulate him on a smooth and orderly transition of power.

'Nothing has yet happened,' she wrote, 'of which the Party would have to be ashamed. Our opponents will be won over to our cause more by the behaviour of Party members than they could be by force ...'

As with all zealous converts to a cult, they imagined that non-believers were to be pitied for not being able to share their vision and see their leader as a messiah. In April, Frau Irrgang wrote from Berlin to commend Hitler on the *Anschluss* adding: 'It is to be regretted that some people still remain blind, but they are beyond help, unfortunately.' The use of the word *etwas* ('some') is significant, for by now opposition to the regime had been all but silenced. Those who had expressed opposition had either emigrated or were imprisoned in the first concentration camps.

Munich Agreement

The peak of Hitler's pre-war popularity came with the signing of the Munich Agreement on 30 September 1938, which saw the surrender of the German-speaking region of Czechoslovakia (known as the Sudetenland). In return Hitler gave Britain's prime minister, Neville Chamberlain, an assurance that it would be his 'last territorial claim in Europe'. Chamberlain returned to Britain waving what would prove to be a worthless guarantee of 'peace in our time'. A year later the world would be at war. But that September the German people were as relieved as their neighbours.

On 10 October, an Armenian woman by the name of Mary Albrecht, who had married a German and was now living in Brussels, wrote to convey her gratitude to the man she and millions of her fellow countrymen and women believed had averted another prolonged and bloody war.

> The day will come when all humanity will thank you. Now those of us who live abroad can prove to all enemies, in black and white, that you only seek peace and always only wanted to have peace, so long as this peace is compatible with our conceptions of honour.

Though her neighbours were openly hostile to Hitler and the increasing threat posed by his expanding armed forces, she had encouraged her children to enlist in the Hitler Youth. And she assured her esteemed leader that a framed copy of the agreement now hung in her parlour and that she carried another in her handbag.

A young Viennese mother, Maria Oberhummer, confessed that she had even tried to delay giving birth to her son (born on 18 April) by two days so that he could share his birthday with the Führer. She was overjoyed on hearing that war had been averted with the signing of the Munich Agreement and one wonders if she and millions like her were still so fervently in favour of Hitler a year later, when Germany invaded Poland.

THE REGIME HAD AN UNCOMPROMISING METHOD OF DEALING WITH HITLER'S MORE IMPASSIONED SUPPORTERS. THEY SENT THE GESTAPO TO CALL ON THEM

As Hitler's personal cult grew in the immediate pre-war years, with a succession of bloodless coups that 'restored' German territory to the Reich, so the amount of fan mail and the nature of the sentiments expressed in those letters intensified, giving rise to concerns over the dictator's security.

The regime had an uncompromising method of dealing with Hitler's more impassioned followers. They instructed the Gestapo or the local police to call on the women in question so they could assess the threat they posed to Hitler's life. If they were merely harmless, infatuated admirers, then they would be warned of the consequences of pestering the Führer and that would be the end of the matter, but if they were judged to pose a serious threat they could be committed to an asylum.

When the postman stopped calling

Many women wrote periodically over several years, despite never having received a reply. Some expressed their bitter disappointment at this lack of appreciation, others were resigned to the fact that the object of their infatuation was busy running the war. And with the coming of war the amount of incoming mail declined significantly. In the seven weeks following the invasion of Poland the Reich Chancellery received fewer than 20 letters.

By 1944 there were no more requests for autographed photos and the few poems that arrived extolled the suffering of the German nation whose trial was nearing its end. There were numerous suggestions on how to produce war-winning weapons or improve the efficiency of those in use, not all of them entirely impractical. Fewer than thirty cards were delivered bearing New Year greetings and a single telegram of congratulations was received from a female admirer on the occasion of Hitler's final birthday on 20 April 1945, when he was already resident in the Berlin bunker.

One of the final letters mailed to the besieged and increasingly ailing dictator was written by Friede Nogler of

Dusseldorf, expressing hope for a final victory, but it had been sent to the Berghof in Berchtesgaden in the belief that Hitler would make his last stand at the so-called Alpine Redoubt. In the event, he chose to stay in Berlin, where he committed suicide on 30 April with Eva Braun at his side.

It is sobering to learn that not one of the tens of thousands of letters received between 1933 and 1939 was personally read by Hitler. He was made aware of the more important letters and instructed his staff to issue a brief reply to some of these, but he did not read any of them himself. He didn't deem them worthy of his time.

CHAPTER FOUR

The Dove and the Eagle – Hitler's Valkyries

At first glance the two women seemed very much alike, for they had both taken to the air in the service of the Nazi regime. There were other female pilots in Germany but Hanna Reitsch and Melitta von Stauffenberg were the only ones to serve the Führer as test pilots and the only women to be awarded the title of Flugkapitänin (flight captain).

But it was here that the similarities ended. Melitta was dark and shy, while the extrovert Hanna was blonde and blue-eyed. In fact, Melitta was a Mischling – that is, she was half-Jewish on her father's side, even though she had been raised a Protestant.

Hanna was from the middle classes while the upper-middle-class and better-educated Melitta had married into the aristocratic and anti-Nazi von Stauffenberg family. And whereas Hanna's belief in the Nazi worldview remained unshaken to the end, Melitta was just as passionately opposed to the regime. In fact, she would covertly assist her brother-in-law, Claus von Stauffenberg, in his attempt to assassinate Hitler.

Needless to say, the two women were bitter adversaries. The one thing that united them was their all-consuming love of flying.

Hanna Reitsch and Melitta von Stauffenberg (née Schiller) shared a passion for flying. Both were fearless test pilots and both had been awarded the Iron Cross for their courage and contribution to the war effort. But although they became symbols of the new Germany they were very different personalities and while Hanna embraced the Nazi regime, Melitta came to despise Hitler and all that he stood for.

Although they became bitter rivals, the two women had more in common than they might have cared to admit. Determined to carve out their own careers, they were both single-minded and fiercely independent and they were also driven by a craving for excitement that verged on the reckless. Neither would be dissuaded by the fact that they had been born into a male-dominated world which had pre-determined the role women should play.

> **HANNA WAS FLAMBOYANT, GREGARIOUS AND ENJOYED BEING IN THE LIMELIGHT. MELITTA WAS SERIOUS AND RESERVED**

Hanna was flamboyant, gregarious and relished being in the limelight. She enjoyed the attention she received from being photographed for magazines and filmed for the newsreels, whereas Melitta was serious and reserved. She shrank from the glare of publicity, preferring to immerse herself in research at the German Research Institute for Aviation.

Blond, blue-eyed Hanna was the personification of the Aryan heroine, a twentieth century valkyrie who dreamed of being a fighter pilot, although she knew the Luftwaffe would not permit it. Melitta was a dark-haired *Mischling*, a half-Jew of mixed blood whose father had converted to Christianity. She had been dismissed from the Luftwaffe in 1936 because of her racial origins but was reinstated because she was too valuable as an engineer and test pilot. Although she had married the elder twin brother of Claus von Stauffenberg, who would plant the bomb that maimed Hitler in July 1944, she justified her work for the regime by telling herself that she was saving the lives of dive-bomber crews, who would be flying in safer planes thanks to the risks she had taken on their behalf.

The magic of flying

It was the era of the glamorous pioneering female aviatrix. Women like Amelia Earhart, who broke a number of records in the 1920s during a career leading up to her solo flight across the Atlantic in 1932. Then there was Mary, Lady Heath, who in 1928 was the first pilot to fly a light aircraft from Cape Town to London, and Amy Johnson, whose epic flight in 1930 made her the first woman to fly solo from England to Australia.

But if the majority of young girls were content to read about the solo flights of these celebrities in glossy society magazines, adorn themselves in fashionable aviatrix accessories and anoint themselves with 'En Avion' perfume, Melitta and Hanna wanted to experience the exhilaration of piloting their own planes.

'Flying exerted an irresistible magic on me,' Melitta enthused. 'I was dominated all along by the longing for freedom.'

Melitta had been born into a respectable, upper-middle-class family, whose daughters were expected to marry well and then settle for cosy domesticity. But she

defied convention by enrolling at the Technical University in Munich to study aeronautical engineering. Hanna, nine years her junior, was a middle-class girl, a doctor's daughter who dropped out of college to devote her time to gliding and attaining her pilot's licence as a means of earning a living. By the early 1930s both would be sufficiently proficient to come to the attention of the Nazi leadership and be chosen to demonstrate their extraordinary aerobatic skills at the Berlin Olympics in 1936. Two years later, Hanna would wow the crowd at the capital's Motor Show, by flying a helicopter inside the exhibition hall, the first woman in the world to fly the new wingless machine.

But instead of becoming allies, the two women became bitter adversaries, avoiding and denigrating each other at every opportunity. Hanna carped that Melitta's achievements were 'unremarkable' and that her Iron Cross was unmerited. But Melitta's passion for flying was in her blood. Her uncle Ernst Eberstein was a First World War ace whose tales of chivalric combat in the skies over Germany had enthralled his niece from an early age. But her romantic dreams of becoming a 'knight of the air' ran parallel to her interest in science. As a schoolgirl, she rigged up an electric light in her attic room so that she could read her physics books all through the night.

Melitta gains her pilot's licence

By the time she graduated from Munich University, Melitta set her sights on obtaining her pilot's licence, although women were prohibited from joining both the Academic Flyers Group and the local flying schools which trained students in engine-powered aircraft. Undaunted, she used her uncle Ernst's name to gain access to one of Germany's greatest living fighter aces, Ernst Udet, and persuaded him to take her up in his two-seater stunt plane during daredevil aerobatic displays.

In 1927, aged 24, she found employment as a flight mechanic and mathematician with DVL, the German Research Institute for Aviation, where her 'meticulous and reliable' approach eventually drew approval from her male colleagues. They also admired her fearlessness, which was not mere bravado but a carefully considered courage which took account of the risks. Within two years she had obtained her pilot's licence, although it required her to travel two hours each way by motorbike from her apartment to the aerodrome before work to rack up the required flying hours.

In 1930 she took part in her first organized flying event where she met two other female pilots, Elly Beinhorn and Marga von Etzdorf. Both were younger and came from privileged families which had financed their daughters' 'hobbies'. Elly was gaining an international reputation for long-distance solo flights, which were seen as public demonstrations of Germany's mastery of the new technology, and would complete a circumnavigation of the world in 1932. Marga owned her own canary yellow aeroplane, in which she had entered the first German Women's Aerobatic Championship earlier that year. She had also made long-distance flights to Morocco, Spain and Sicily and would complete a solo flight to Japan, which would make her an international celebrity. But it would be Hanna and Melitta who would make the most enduring impression during the 1930s and 1940s and become known as 'the women who flew for Hitler'.

Aristocratic marriage

At a high society family wedding the following year Melitta met her future husband, Alexander von Stauffenberg, a tall intellectual with a poetic sensibility who distanced himself from the rabid National Socialists among the aristocracy. He admired her energy and respected her single-minded determination to realize her dreams, regardless of the considerable obstacles placed in her path.

Their marriage in 1937 brought her into the midst of an old Prussian family who considered themselves to be the custodians of a noble tradition which prided itself on loyalty to the Church, the state, the monarchy and the military. They viewed the rise of the rabble-rouser Hitler and his thugs as an affront to their culture and spiritual values. But the Communists posed an even greater threat to their way of life. Though the Nazis' extreme nationalism and brown-shirted paramilitary were abhorrent to a proud, disciplined aristocracy, they conceded that desperate times called for desperate measures. The National Socialists would stem the red tide which the democratic government of the Weimar Republic was seemingly impotent to control. If the red revolution were to succeed, it would create instability and chaos as it had done in Russia less than 15 years earlier and would almost certainly see the Stauffenbergs stripped of their wealth and title. Melitta was now an adopted member of a noble elite and as such would have to weather the storm with the rest of her new family.

Hanna's first flight

In 1931 Melitta's future rival Hanna Reitsch was 19 years old. The pretty and petite daughter of affluent middle-class parents, who had grown up in Hirschberg, eastern Germany, had just made her first flight at the Grunau Gliding School, wheeling like a bird over the same fertile valleys that Melitta had flown over a few years earlier.

It was a dream come true for the girl who had habitually launched herself into space from trees of increasingly precarious heights as a child, in the certainty that she could fly. It was only after fracturing her skull that she was forced to admit that she might require an artificial aid to defy gravity, much to the relief of her parents, who held on to the hope that she might grow out of her unladylike ambitions. But Hanna was wilful and persistent. She eventually struck a bargain with her father which obliged him to pay for glider lessons if she passed her school graduation exam, the dreaded *Arbitur*.

Her first flight was exhilarating but it ended with a dramatic crash. Neither glider nor pilot were injured, however, and Hanna earned the admiration of her fellow students, among whom was the future Nazi rocket scientist Wernher von Braun, who complimented her on her daring. She passed further test flights with flying colours, though she had to repeat the first test because the assessor had attributed her success to luck. It was apparently easier for a woman to master the skills required to fly than to overcome the ingrained prejudices of the men who trained them.

But skilled pilots were in short supply and in 1932 Hanna was offered the opportunity to test-fly a new glider. Her five-hour flight set a new world record for female glider pilots and this earned her a rapturous reception throughout the country.

Hanna later claimed to have no interest in politics, but it could not have escaped her notice that 1932 was the year Hitler too was making headlines, campaigning by air for the first time in history so that he could speak at up to five political rallies a day at opposite ends of the country.

Breaking the altitude barrier

Hanna had grown up during the years of hyperinflation, mass unemployment and civil unrest, in an atmosphere of uncertainty and spontaneous violence. Her parents had been quick to blame the Allies for Germany's plight, the Weimar government for not contesting their punitive reparation bill and a mythical global Jewish cabal for everything else that was wrong with the world at that time. It led her to see Hitler as the strong man Germany needed and to choose to ignore the ugly aspect of his extremist nationalist politics, as he enforced his party's racist policies with ballot rigging backed up by brute force. Hanna was too self-absorbed to be distracted by what was happening around her, specifically Hitler's succession to the Chancellorship in January 1933, the suppression of all political opposition after the Nazi-orchestrated Reichstag fire in February and the passing of the Enabling Act in May, which legitimized the dictatorship.

That turbulent spring, she had eyes for only one thing – the Schneider Grunau Baby, the latest training glider, which boasted a blind-flying control panel enabling the pilot to navigate through thick clouds and fog. Inevitably, she persuaded the inventor to allow her to take a trial flight and could not resist testing herself and the new machine to the limit. Instead of cruising at a safe height she sought out an ominous black storm cloud and lost herself in it.

Within minutes the blissful feeling of disconnectedness was shattered by the furious pounding of hailstones puncturing the fuselage and the cracking of the cockpit canopy as ice rendered her blind. Punching a hole in the cabin window she attempted to manipulate the frozen joystick, but found her hands turning blue with the cold. She was also in danger of passing out from lack of oxygen. The situation was not helped by the fact that she was only wearing a light summer dress and sandals, as the flight was unplanned. Miraculously she managed to regain control but only by allowing the glider to plunge nose down towards the ground.

When she finally landed, she found herself in the Neutral Zone near the Czechoslovakian border and in breach of international law. But once again, her reckless audacity had netted her another world record – for breaking the altitude barrier in a single-seater engineless glider. Her border violation was excused in the excitement.

Working for the regime

Both Hanna and Melitta rose to public prominence at the same time as their future benefactor Adolf Hitler, who would capitalize on the public's love affair with glamorous aviatrices for propaganda purposes. The regime and its cronies shamelessly exploited these women as Melitta was to learn that May, when her friend Marga von Etzdorf was caught with banned weapons aboard her plane. Marga had been forced to land in French-occupied Syria during an aborted flight to Australia and was found to be in violation of the Versailles Treaty by carrying a prototype machine gun and sales literature on behalf of a German weapons manufacturer. Rather than face imprisonment by the French authorities, Marga shot herself. Her needless suicide grieved Melitta, who became embittered and blamed the Nazis for having cynically used her friend, who had only agreed to carry the illicit cargo because she needed the money.

> **ADOLF HITLER WOULD CAPITALIZE ON THE PUBLIC'S LOVE AFFAIR WITH GLAMOROUS AVIATRICES FOR PROPAGANDA PURPOSES**

With the passing of the infamous Nuremberg Laws in 1935, the dictatorship made its insidious racist ideology official government policy. Melitta had no illusions about what this would mean for her father's fellow Jews or for herself, if she should cease to be of use to the regime. She now kept silent on matters relating to her family, resisted the temptation to discuss politics with her colleagues at DVL and worked long and diligently to ensure that she became indispensable to the institute and its official government sponsor.

The new administration provided equipment and seemingly unlimited funds for research and test flights, though these were now clearly made with a military application in mind. Her work measuring the stress on propellers and improving dive-brakes would be a significant contribution to the effectiveness of the Stuka dive-bombers, which would spearhead the invasion of Poland in 1939 and the blitzkrieg in the spring of 1940. But the work was not without its risks as thirteen of her colleagues were killed in the process.

Racist Olympics

During this period, Hanna was actively involved in testing prototype gliders at Darmstadt while attending the Civil Airways Training School at Stettin, which was a military base in all but name. She was required to drill in a uniform several sizes too large for her petite figure, to the amusement of the other students, who were all male. And when she climbed into the cockpit of a Focke-Wulf Fw 44 or a Heinkel reconnaissance plane, she had to bolster the seat with cushions to reach the controls. But if her colleagues found her presence a novelty, the public admired her and avidly followed her exploits in the glossy magazines. She even acquired a coterie of admirers, who would keep a scrapbook of cuttings and treasure the latest addition to the 'Modern Beauties' cigarette card collection, which depicted her attired in fur-collared flying jacket and framed in gold.

Although both women were aware of the other's work and had several mutual friends they refused to acknowledge each other in public. Whether this was due to political differences, class snobbery, personal animosity or plain old professional jealousy is not known. But it is likely that Melitta objected to what she saw as Hanna's frivolous, devil-may-care attitude and blatant narcissism, while Hanna would have found Melitta's sense of entitlement and air of intellectual superiority condescending and hard to bear. Melitta could not summon up much respect for someone who appeared to have acquired a reputation without having earned it through study and hard work. It all seemed to come too easily to Hanna, who had no understanding of aeronautical engineering and was now being feted as a symbol of the regime.

It must also have been galling for Melitta, the *Mischling*, to see that the eyes of the world were so blind to what was taking place in Germany under the Nazis. The only athletes of Jewish origin chosen for the German team were the fencer Helene Mayer – who was granted the dubious privilege of being an 'honorary Aryan' for the day because she was the best chance the Germans had of winning a medal in that particular sport – and track star Gretel Bergmann, who had been cheated out of her rightful place by her own team. The Nazis had tried to sideline Bergmann by pairing her with a man posing as a female, because they could not bear the thought that a Jew might prove the superior athlete, even if she won a medal for Germany. As a result, she was quietly dropped from the team at the last moment.

The international press appeared oblivious to the deception and the host nation's betrayal of the Olympic ideal, so dazzled were they by the spectacle stage-managed by the regime. They took their cue from the *Olympia Zeitung*, the official organ of the games, which trumpeted that 'the biggest victor of the games was Adolf Hitler'. The Führer's celebrity guests were in agreement. Charles Lindbergh, the American aviator, condemned Germany's critics and blamed the Jews for their own misfortune, which he attributed to their support for the Communists. He flattered the dictator in the newsreels and the press, calling Hitler 'a great man', while his wife called Hitler 'a visionary'.

Death-defying Olympics stunt

The Olympics of 1936 were a public relations coup for the Nazis, who were openly flaunting their military muscle having remilitarized the Rhineland that spring in defiance of the Versailles Treaty. They were now waging a propaganda war to soften up the isolationists and intimidate their neighbours in readiness for the bloodless coups that Hitler was already planning behind the scenes. Within two years his army would cross the border to occupy Austria and portions of Czechoslovakia, as a prelude to the invasion of Poland.

Hanna was being openly courted by the regime now that the Luftwaffe had been recognized as being the official German air force and rearmament was an open secret. That summer she was given the honorary title of Flugkapitänin and presented with the combined Pilot's and Observer's Badge in gold with diamonds by Reichsmarschall Goering, together with an auto-graphed photograph of her 'chief' which he dedicated to 'The Captain of the Air, Hanna Reitsch'. She was then just 25 years old and had 2,000 hours in the air to her credit.

> **HANNA WAS PRESENTED WITH THE PILOT'S AND OBSERVER'S BADGE IN GOLD WITH DIAMONDS BY REICHSMARSCHALL GOERING**

But it was Melitta who would take the honours on the day before the opening ceremony in July 1936, when the eyes of the world were on Nazi Germany and its stable of Aryan athletes. The Olympiade Grossflugtag was held at Tempelhof airfield and proved to be a memorable day of aerial displays and aerobatics, during which Melitta performed a spectac-ular death-defying stunt in a stripped-down Heinkel bomber to the delight of tens of thousands of spectators, among whom was Hitler himself. It did not, however, save her from being discharged from her workplace for making disparaging remarks about the regime and for her suspect heritage, although the official reason given for her dismissal was that she had made an unauthorized flight to Hungary.

Before the end of the year she would find employment with Askania, a leading aeronautical engineering company in Berlin, but she was under no illusion about the gyroscopic and navigational instruments that she was helping to develop. They were to be used for military purposes. As she once told a colleague: 'War is already predetermined … It will come to a terrible end.'

Hanna was recruited as a military test pilot and naively regarded the warplanes at Rechlin airbase where she was assigned as 'guardians at the portal of Peace'.

Testing dive-bombers

The Nazis were masters of doublespeak and deceit. They presented their unjustified and unprovoked invasion of Poland in September 1939 as 'the Defensive Campaign' and most of the population accepted it as such without question. Melitta was not so easily fooled, but it would have been fatal to voice dissent. All she could do was bide her time and hope that some of Hitler's disaffected and horrified generals might attempt a coup. In the meantime, she immersed herself in her work, dividing her time between test flights and the drawing board. It was a gruelling period in her life that few men could have sustained.

Testing dive-bombers was physically exhausting. She would enter an almost vertical dive from 1,370 metres (4,000 feet) at speeds of up to 560kph (350mph), when the plane would shake so violently that she couldn't read the instruments. She would then release her cement bombs just 150–200 metres (500–650 feet) from the ground before pulling back on the joystick and bringing her Junkers level at 6g – the crucial point at which pilots could succumb to loss of consciousness. Several of her fellow test pilots suffered bouts of uncontrollable vomiting during and after such tests and others crashed before they could bail out. In a fast dive, blood would rush to the pilot's head causing 'red-out', which affected vision and caused blood vessels in the eyes to burst. Pulling out of a dive too quickly would cause the blood to drain from the head resulting in black-outs, a reaction Melitta suffered on several occasions but from which she managed to recover just in time.

Her former sponsor, the First World War flying ace Ernst Udet, was so exhausted after a couple of dive-bomber test flights that he had to be helped out of his chair after a rest in the officer's mess. Melitta flew up to fifteen such tests a day and in between she would make her calculations without the aid of modern instruments, often working late into the night before resuming early the next morning.

She repeatedly refused to allow other pilots to conduct the tests, not only believing that it was wrong to put their lives at risk to obtain the data she needed but also because she wanted to experience the effects of fast dives for herself. Gender had long ceased to be an issue for Melitta, who would tell a conference in Stockholm in autumn 1943 that she and her fellow aviatrices were not 'suffragettes'.

Giant gliders

Hanna meanwhile, was contributing to the development of larger, troop-carrying noiseless gliders. They were deployed for the first time during the assault on the Dutch border fortress of Eben-Emael in May 1940, when 42 gliders carrying commandos were launched from an airport in Cologne. After the successful assault on the fortress, plans were drawn up for an aerial invasion of England, utilizing a new giant wood and steel glider which could carry heavy weapons, 200 troops or an armoured vehicle. It would be powered by three liquid-fuelled rocket engines affixed to the wings and would be towed to the landing zone by three engine-powered planes flying in synchronized formation. The Messerschmitt Me 321 'Gigant' was to be designed using Hanna's expertise and experience, but her superiors were extremely reluctant to allow her to fly it, fearing that she was not strong enough to handle the heavier controls.

She was not easily dissuaded and eventually secured a test flight, though adjustments had to be made to accommodate her diminutive frame. Wooden blocks were placed on the rudder pedal and a cushion pushed her forward in the pilot's seat. But more significantly she was accompanied by a back-up crew, one of whom took over the controls when she found it difficult to land the immense machine.

It was an ill-fated project and no pilot could be sure of bringing it down safely. In a subsequent test the Gigant crashed, killing the six-man crew as well as the pilots of the three

NO PILOT COULD BE SURE OF BRINGING THE MESSERSCHMITT ME 321 'GIGANT' DOWN SAFELY. IN A SUBSEQUENT TEST, IT CRASHED KILLING THE SIX-MAN CREW

towing planes. It was only after another fatal accident, which saw the deaths of all four crews and the 110 troops aboard the glider, that the project was reluctantly cancelled.

Other prototypes were tested and one almost cost Hanna her life as she attempted to land on the deck of a warship only to be ensnared in cables. Another perilous test flight required Hanna to sit in the cockpit of a pilotless glider which had been developed as a means of refuelling aeroplanes in flight. The controls were fixed and so without a means of piloting the unstable aircraft she was forced to sit and endure its violent shaking until she experienced 'the most primitive and hateful fear'. She was then ordered to fly a customized bomber into the steel cables of a barrage balloon to test its effectiveness in severing the cables, which were the bane of night bomber crews as they could not be seen in the dark. A heavy fender had been riveted to the nose of Hanna's prototype bomber to deflect the cables on to razor sharp blades affixed to the wing tips. She must have seen her role as no longer that of a regular test pilot but a human guinea pig sent to carry out suicidal experiments. The barrage balloon experiment was yet another sign of desperation by the Luftwaffe, who had lost the Führer's confidence and their former prestige after their failure to win the Battle of Britain in the summer of 1940

– a failure Goering attempted to blame on his subordinate, Ernst Udet.

Incredibly, the barrage balloon experiment was repeated the following spring after the fender had been replaced with an oversized steel blade. When Hanna's plane hit the cable, it coiled into the air, sending shards of propeller through the cockpit window. Miraculously, Hanna was unharmed and managed to bring the crippled bomber down safely, to the astonishment of the assembled witnesses, among them Udet, now the Luftwaffe's Director General of Equipment. Udet would commit suicide that autumn after blaming Goering for betraying him and abandoning him to his enemies within the regime. But at this point he still had some influence with Hitler.

A few weeks after her near-death experience with the barrage balloon Hanna travelled to Berlin where she was awarded the Iron Cross, Second Class for valour, making her the first woman to be awarded the coveted medal. Hitler greeted her 'with friendly warmth', while Goering stood to one side beaming like a proud father who had been 'permitted to introduce a prettily mannered child'. The two men listened as she regaled them with details of her recent exploits, illustrating her stories with sweeping arm movements like a fighter ace demonstrating his latest kill for his squadron in the mess.

German blood certificate

The war was not yet turning against the aggressor, but the portents were there for those who could read them. For all her commitment and painstaking calculations, Melitta was grieved to hear that German pilots and crews were dying at an alarming rate. The Stuka pilots were proving to be easy targets for British anti-aircraft gunners, who could predict their trajectory once they went into a dive and blast them out of the air before they had a chance to release their bombs. These once terrifying weapons would be used with less frequency and were practically phased out altogether before the tide turned. German bomber crews were also suffering heavy losses. They were easy prey for RAF fighters and anti-aircraft fire as they flew over Britain's cities, their appearance anticipated by radar and their flight path plotted by Fighter Command. Added to that, their fighter escorts did not have the capability to remain over their target for sufficiently long to protect them from the swarms of Spitfires and Hurricanes and the bombers themselves were inadequately armed.

In June 1941, Melitta's contribution to the war effort was officially acknowledged by Goering, who approved the issuing of her 'Declaration of German Blood' (*Deutschblütigkeitserklärung*). It ended years of uncertainty for her, but not for her father and siblings. At the risk of having her own status revoked, she applied for certificates for her family, knowing that only a tiny proportion of applications had been successful. Her gamble paid off, but this life-saving loophole would soon be closed.

Melitta continued to risk her life a dozen times a day during dive-bombing flight tests, but according to Max Escher, her husband's friend, she was now also under extreme mental stress knowing that she was serving a criminal regime.

While Melitta continued to push herself beyond the limits, Hanna was becoming less exacting and was exhibiting the more unpleasant aspects of her newly acquired celebrity. Her insistence on having unfettered access to prototypes frequently led to costly delays in testing these aeroplanes and her colleagues were now openly criticizing her for being in too much of a hurry to approve aircraft that were subsequently found to have significant defects.

One pilot remarked bitterly that she flew 'with her heart and not with her brains' and 'without critical understanding of her work'. Her arrogance prohibited her from asking the advice of her male colleagues, to whom she appeared haughty and condescending, and her continual insistence on being the first to fly a new prototype angered her fellow pilots. As if to compensate for not having been taken seriously by her male colleagues, she now proclaimed her superiority by affecting an imperious attitude. And while no one could say that she had not earned their admiration and respect as a pilot, her lack of technical knowledge and refusal to cooperate as a member of the group was considered a serious weakness.

Sexual orientation rumours

Although Hanna claimed to be the girlfriend of Waffen SS commando Otto Skorzeny, it is likely that she did so only to keep her amorous male colleagues at bay. It may also have been a way of squashing rumours that she was attracted to her own sex, which might explain why she expressed a melodramatic revulsion towards homosexuality whenever Melitta was mentioned. Hanna's former glider teacher, Peter Riedel, witnessed an angry outburst in December 1941 during which his former pupil accused her rival of having made unwanted advances; she also alluded to her Jewish heritage using 'crude' and 'ugly' terms, insulting Melitta 'in the nastiest' way'. 'This was the first time Hanna Reitsch disappointed me as a person,' Riedel remarked.

Hanna may have been a disappointment to her former teacher, but her superiors saw her as the personification of Aryan heroism. Even so, they had no hesitation in using her to test a plane which had already claimed the lives of several pilots. Her latest assignment in the winter of 1942 was to put the Messerschmitt Me163 Komet rocket-powered fighter through its paces and see where its weaknesses lay. The Komet was capable of reaching speeds of up to 500mph in seconds and an altitude of 30,000 feet, but after a few minutes its fuel was spent and it would glide back down to earth, landing at up to 150mph. The plane was a potential flying bomb due to its combustible mixture of methanol and hydrogen peroxide fuel stored in tanks to the side and back of the cockpit. On one occasion, the fatal mixture had leaked into the cockpit, eating through the pilot's acid-resistant suit and dissolving his right arm and his head. According to the flight engineer, they had been reduced to 'a mass of soft jelly'.

Mission impossible

Hanna knew the dangers before she strapped herself into the cockpit for her first flight, having witnessed an earlier test when the plane exploded into a fireball before her eyes, incinerating the pilot. She had also heard of others who had been killed when it exploded in mid-air or on landing, which was a particularly hazardous procedure as a jolt could ignite any unspent fuel. She was only given the opportunity to fly the Komet because her predecessor, Heini Dittmar, had suffered spinal injuries when landing, when the shock of impact was transmitted to his seat after the undercarriage failed to extend properly. Hanna was deemed to be the only pilot with the necessary nerve and experience to take his place.

The urgent need to put a new super plane into production at this stage of the war overcame all reservations the Luftwaffe and the High Command may have had concerning the safety of one of its most high-profile heroes.

Hanna's first flight in the war-winning super plane was an unqualified success and she later described the sensation as comparable to 'sitting on a cannonball'. But after crashing on her fifth flight in a prototype carrying water ballast instead of fuel, she was severely injured and given little chance of survival. Fearing that their female Icarus had finally run out of luck, her superiors petitioned Hitler to award her the Iron Cross First Class while there was still time. She became the first woman to wear that prestigious medal.

Meeting 'the Fat Man'

Melitta received her Iron Cross Second Class in January 1943 when she was summoned to Goering's villa in Berlin, where the Reichsmarschall expressed his 'deep, sincere admiration' for her achievements. If Melitta had expected to be received with cold formality she was pleasurably mistaken. 'The Fat Man', as he was commonly known, exhibited an 'honest and touching heartiness', while Emmy Goering offered her and Alexander the use of their private box at the theatre and invited the couple to stay as their guests whenever they wished. Emmy may not have been aware that Melitta was a *Mischling*, or may have justified her presence on the grounds that she was now officially an Aryan, but the Reichsmarschall had a pragmatic attitude, once declaring that he would decide who was a Jew and who was not. The Reich had need of this *Halbjuden* and that was the end of the matter.

It is significant that in her official portrait photo taken by Hitler's personal photographer Heinrich Hoffmann, Melitta conceals the medal under her jacket to hide the swastika. Only the ribbon is visible and that is bound in a decorative bow.

Goering's fantasy world

Hanna spent five months in hospital after her near-fatal crash, during which time she was subjected to lengthy operations to reconstruct her face. When she was finally released, she began a protracted and isolated convalescence. By the time she had recovered sufficiently to consider flying again, the tide of war had turned against Germany and the Nazi leadership seemed wilfully ignorant of the deteriorating situation. During an informal meeting with Goering at his villa in the Obersalzberg, Hanna was horrified to hear that the head of the Luftwaffe was under the impression that the Me 163 was already rolling off the assembly line. When Hanna attempted to give him a more realistic picture of aircraft production he went into a rage, pounded the table and stormed out of the room. She attributed his tantrum to his morphine addiction, his feminine affectations which included the use of cosmetics and his 'abnormal' size. It was clear to her that he was living in a fantasy from which his trusted attendants were sworn not to disturb him. She was never invited to meet Goering again.

Instead, she attempted to curry favour with Himmler, who had sent her chocolates and a series of handwritten notes during her convalescence. That July she accepted the Reichsführer's invitation to dinner at his East Prussian HQ, followed by a private audience with him in his study afterwards. She found his appearance unexceptional but was disarmed by his good manners and what she described as his affability. If her own memoirs are to be believed, she felt emboldened to question him about his views on marriage and how he reconciled these with the Lebensborn programme. She was told that his views had been either 'misrepresented or misinterpreted'. He intended to establish a women's branch of the SS and hoped that he could rely on her to dispute any similar misconceptions about him when she heard them expressed in the future.

WHEN HANNA ATTEMPTED TO GIVE HIM A MORE REALISTIC PICTURE OF AIRCRAFT PRODUCTION, GOERING STORMED OUT OF THE ROOM

Operation Suicide

By the early autumn of 1943 even Nazi loyalist Hanna had conceded that defeat was imminent. Moreover, she knew that she was not the only one to be thinking the unthinkable. That August at the Berlin Aero Club she voiced her concerns to two trusted friends, Captain Heinrich Lange of the Luftwaffe and Dr Theo Benzinger, the head of Rechlin's institute of aeronautical medicine. They agreed that a

negotiated peace with the Allies was the only way to save Germany from annihilation and another humiliating defeat. All three were of course aware that on 12 February that year President Roosevelt had stipulated that Hitler would have to be removed before the Allies would accept Germany's 'unconditional surrender'. However, Hanna had no intention of conspiring to overthrow her Führer but only of bringing the conflict to a halt while much of Germany was still intact and its industry functioning.

With the German army in retreat in the East and the navy effectively neutralized by Allied air superiority, it was down to the Luftwaffe to force the Allies to agree to a ceasefire so that negotiations could begin. As long as this stalemate could be achieved before the Allies launched their second front in North Africa or Europe, there was a chance to halt the bombing that was crippling German industry, levelling Germany's cities and killing tens of thousands of civilians. They would force the Allies to come to terms by staging a 'succession of devastating blows' against key installations, factories, infrastructure and shipping. Acknowledging their slim chances of returning alive, Hanna suggested that they give their last-ditch stand the codename Operation Suicide.

Such defeatist talk was punishable by death. Every week as many as a hundred civilians were sentenced to death by Nazi courts for expressing such opinions or for acts of sabotage, which in practice meant mere criticism of the regime. No one voicing such thoughts was immune from prosecution. Not even those whose courage had been rewarded with an Iron Cross.

Despite Hanna's insistence on absolute secrecy, rumours of her proposed martyrdom reached Melitta, who was frequently heard to refer to her rival thereafter as Saint Joan. Hanna later claimed that she soon attracted an encouraging number of pilots who were willing to sacrifice their lives for their Fatherland but was thwarted by Field

Marshal Erhard Milch, who informed her that he couldn't afford to lose either pilots or their planes in such a fool-hardy and dubious operation.

Morale-boosting tour

That November Hanna was reassigned to a morale-boosting tour of the Eastern Front, where it was hoped her presence would stiffen the resolve of the beleaguered troops. There she experienced the bitter cold of a Russian winter and cowered in a foxhole during a Russian artillery barrage. Deprived of sleep night after night as the guns shook the earth all around, she came to appreciate what the infantry were suffering for weeks and months on end. What they really needed were reinforcements, winter clothing and supplies, not a flying visit from an ever-smiling Nazi poster girl. But Hanna, as ever, was oblivious to reality. She wrote that their eyes lit up at the sight of her and that they were determined to fight on after she told them about the top secret 'wonder weapons' – the V1, V2 and Me 163 – that were about to go into production. Doubtless some may have believed their own propaganda, but there must have been many who wondered if history was repeating itself. With the Luftwaffe grounded by the severe weather, preventing supplies from getting through, and the defeat at Stalingrad a fresh open wound, their fitful dreams must have been haunted by images of Napoleon's troops dying by the dozen on the road back from Moscow.

Hitler's decline

On 28 February 1944, Hanna made an official visit to the Berghof to receive the certificate confirming the award of her Iron Cross, which she had received a year earlier. She took the opportunity to seek Hitler's approval for Operation Suicide, thereby circumventing both Goering and Milch. To her consternation, she found the Führer prematurely aged and ill-tempered. He did not believe that the situation warranted such desperate measures and was soon immersed in another of his interminable monologues, citing numerous historical events when victory was snatched from the jaws of imminent defeat. His new secret weapons would win the war at the eleventh hour and bring the Allies to their knees.

There was clearly no arguing or reasoning with him when he was in this frame of mind. It was a practised strategy of his to silence unwanted discussion. Hanna thought his chosen examples were 'irrelevant' and was bitterly disappointed not to have gained his approval, nor to have her willingness to sacrifice herself acknowledged. 'Hitler,' she later observed, 'was living in some remote and nebulous world of his own.' When she attempted to enlighten him on the facts regarding production of the new wonder weapons, she was told that she was misinformed.

Hanna was nothing if not persistent and pressed Hitler to at least consent to her making preliminary preparations, to which he grudgingly and half-heartedly agreed. On returning to her duties at the aeronautical research institute she immediately began drawing up revised plans for what had now been renamed Operation Self-Sacrifice.

Goebbels reacted to the news of Hanna's proposed plan in characteristic fashion.

'You shouldn't let women be the lead advocate dealing with such important questions,' he confided to his diary. 'Even with all their efforts, their sense of intelligence will fail, and men, especially of high calibre, would have difficulties allowing themselves to follow the lead of a woman.'

If she imagined that the leadership would applaud her idea, she was cruelly disillusioned when Himmler suggested replacing experienced pilots with 'the incurably diseased, neurotics and criminals'.

Operation Valkyrie

On 21 May 1944, Melitta was approached by her brother-in-law Claus von Stauffenberg and asked to participate in Operation Valkyrie, the assassination of Adolf Hitler. She did not hesitate to give her consent. The plan was for her to fake an emergency landing at the Führer's headquarters and fly Claus back to Berlin to coordinate the *coup d'état*. In the event, Melitta's assistance was not required because the conspirators elected to use another pilot. She was fortunate not to be involved because the assassination was foiled by a series of those unpredictable quirks of fate that invariably derail the best-laid plans.

After two aborted attempts on 11 and 15 July, which had to be called off because two of the intended targets, Himmler and Goering, failed to show up, it was decided that the third attempt must proceed no matter what. It seemed unlikely that they would get another opportunity to eliminate what Stauffenberg referred to as the 'psychopaths' dragging his country to the edge of the abyss.

July 20 was a stifling hot day and so the venue for Hitler's daily briefing was changed to a wooden hut with raised steel shutters and open windows, thereby diffusing the intensity of the explosion. The time bomb, which had been placed in von Stauffenberg's briefcase, was only half the strength it should have been as there had not been time to prime both packets of explosive before he was ushered into the meeting. And perhaps most crucially, the briefcase was moved after von Stauffenberg left the room to answer a prearranged phone call. When it exploded, the concrete table support deflected the full force of the blast, leaving Hitler with only minor injuries.

Stauffenberg and the ring leaders were quickly rounded up and summarily shot which incensed Hitler, who had wanted to prolong their suffering by having them executed by slow strangulation using piano wire. He was also denied the perverse pleasure of having their executions filmed for his subsequent gratification. In his rage, he ordered the death of up to 5,000 people, some of whom committed suicide rather than suffer the indignity of a Nazi show trial. A vindictive Hitler then ordered Claus's body to be exhumed and burned and 'the whole brood' liquidated. That included Melitta, who was arrested by the Gestapo and imprisoned in their formidable headquarters on Prinz-Albrecht-Strasse.

Imprisonment and release

It took all of Melitta's courage and resourcefulness to survive those first few days and nights in the cell from which she was sure she would be taken one morning, stood up against a wall and shot. To keep her sanity, she devised a routine which included exercise, washing and mending her clothes. She had managed to smuggle her diary into the prison, in which she wrote: 'Think a lot of the dead. Maybe I'll see them soon.'

After six weeks' confinement, first at Gestapo HQ and then at Charlottenburg prison, she was released following a concerted campaign on her behalf by her fellow pilots and SS officer Paul Opitz, who had been assigned to investigate the plot. It is likely that Opitz was eager to ally himself to an anti-Nazi who might speak for him after the war, as he expected to be prosecuted for acting as an administrator of the Einsatzgruppen mass murders in Poland. Goering granted Melitta's release on the grounds that her work was vital to the war effort and on condition that she no longer used the Stauffenberg name, which was to be erased from the history books and all public records.

RETURNING TO WORK, MELITTA HAD ONLY ONE THING ON HER MIND – THE RELEASE OF HER HUSBAND AND OTHER MEMBERS OF THE STAUFFENBERG FAMILY

From the day she returned to work, Melitta had only one thing on her mind – the release of her husband and other members of the Stauffenberg family. Under the Nazi's *Sippenhaft* dictum, by which all members of a family or group are punished for the actions of one of their number, even the children and grandchildren had been rounded up. The older children were transported to concentration camps and the younger ones were taken to an orphanage. By day Melitta divided her time between training pilots in night-flying techniques and lobbying various government departments to have her relatives released. At night, she flew in the dark to test blind-flying equipment. As one of her friends remarked, there seemed to be no time when she slept.

Germany's would-be suicide pilots

Hanna, meanwhile, had managed to assemble a 70-strong group of volunteers willing to lay down their lives for Führer and Fatherland in what would surely have been a futile, melodramatic gesture of defiance. In the event, they were not required to make the ultimate sacrifice. More significantly, Hanna had advanced plans to adapt the destructive V1 rocket for manned flight, effectively making the weapon a guided bomb, but the tests were plagued with fatal or near fatal accidents that demonstrated its unsuitability for manned flight and Hanna was reduced to tears of frustration when the Air Ministry cancelled further tests. Ignoring the order, she continued testing the V1 until she had ironed out all of the imperfections and solved various technical problems by trial and error, surviving a series of rough landings and other difficulties that would have proved fatal to inexperienced pilots. But her sheer bloody-mindedness, resourcefulness and unquestionable courage carried her through.

However, it was all in vain. When the Allies landed in Normandy on 6 June 1944 the window of opportunity for both Operation Self-Sacrifice and the piloted V1 was closed. Hanna's 70 pilots were recalled to their posts and work on the manned rocket was shut down.

Even at this late hour she remained a committed National Socialist and would hear nothing against the Party.

When she met Peter Riedel again in September she had evidently been seduced by Himmler's unctuous charm and spoke of him as a 'kind, good-natured man' who was 'quite compassionate and charming'. When Peter produced photographic evidence of the mass killings at Majdanek concentration camp, she angrily dismissed it as enemy propaganda, to which Peter responded by demanding to know where the 800,000 pairs of shoes in one photograph had come from and why the international press had reprinted the accusations against the regime if it was nothing but Communist lies. He said that she should show the material to Himmler if she was so certain that the Reichsführer SS was 'an honourable man' and they parted after she had agreed to do just that.

Mission to rescue Hitler

If Hanna's account of her meeting with Himmler is to be believed – for she was economical with the truth in her self-glorifying memoirs – he remained impassive as he examined the documents Peter had given her, refusing to comment. Instead he asked Hanna if she believed the accusations, to which she replied firmly that she certainly did not. She suggested that he make a public statement countering the claims, which were now circulating in the foreign press, but he made no such commitment. She would just have to judge the alleged evidence for herself, he said. Hanna left the meeting relieved and reassured, although she had not received the emphatic denial she had hoped for. But it was sufficient to assuage her conscience.

Hanna shared her Führer's delusions to the end. In January 1945, after the Allies had demonstrated that they had total air supremacy by destroying 250 German planes when the Luftwaffe made an unsuccessful attempt to bomb Allied airfields, she told Otto Skorzeny: 'I shall soon be in the thick of it again.'

But there was nothing for her to do other than to

plan her final gesture of loyalty to the regime – the rescue of Hitler from his besieged bunker in Berlin. A mission of such importance had to be authorized by the Luftwaffe's most senior officer, former First World War fighter ace Robert Ritter von Greim, who would become the final commander of the German air force following Goering's dismissal. Greim had complete faith in Hanna's ability to fly almost anything with wings, but flying under fire on what was likely to be a suicide mission was something he could not delegate to a subordinate. He insisted on piloting the plane himself, reducing Hanna to the role of navigator.

Flight across Berlin

On 21 April, the day after the Führer's birthday, the Russian artillery bombardment of Berlin began. In the east of the capital, the noise of the guns was so loud that the vibrations caused telephones to ring in empty offices and furniture to move by itself.

Himmler, Goering and Speer fled the city, leaving Hitler with vague assurances of their undying loyalty. Only Goebbels and Martin Bormann remained among the group of functionaries, secretaries and staff officers who still looked to their Führer for leadership, believing that as long as he lived there was still a chance that they too might survive.

Hanna and Greim had hoped to fly the helicopter prototype from the Berlin district of Gatow to the Brandenburg Gate and land in front of the Chancellery, but it had been destroyed in an air raid and so they were forced to take a light Storch observation plane instead. The single-seater aircraft allowed for only one pilot, so Hanna had to stand behind Greim without a seat belt to secure her as he took evasive action, wheeling sharply to avoid enemy fighters. When they reached the Grunewald, the forested area on the outskirts of the city, they flew so low that they could see the upturned faces of the Soviet soldiers taking aim with their rifles. When Greim was hit, Hanna took the controls by leaning over the unconscious pilot as the aircraft was rocked by explosions.

Petrol was now leaking into the cockpit from both damaged engines and smoke and fumes had reduced visibility to practically nil, but she managed to land safely in the vicinity of the Victory Column. It must surely have been her most extraordinary flight.

Berlin was unrecognizable. If it had not been for the column and a few other landmarks, she might have been anywhere. The surreal landscape, combined with lack of sleep and the ordeal she had just been through, left Hanna in a daze which became all the more dreamlike when she met Hitler.

A broken man

In the 'deeply depressing' stillness of the bunker, she found her Führer a broken man, his head hanging down, his arms convulsively twitching, his eyes 'glassy and remote' and his voice expressionless. As Greim lay in agony on a stretcher, Hitler took his hands and then turned to Hanna to commend her on her courage and loyalty.

'Nothing is spared me! Nothing!' he ranted. 'Every disillusion, every betrayal, dishonour, treason has been heaped upon me.'

He then told her that he had just had Goering placed under house arrest in his villa at the Obersalzberg for 'shameless treachery' in assuming command while his Führer still lived and for attempting to negotiate a surrender with the Allies. Hitler now appointed the wounded and prostrate Greim Field Marshal and Commander of the Luftwaffe in his place. He could have conferred this dubious honour by phone, but in summoning Greim to Berlin it was clear that he wanted his most loyal servants by his side when the empire that he had boasted would last a thousand years went up in flames, as if playing out the last act of Richard Wagner's *Götterdämmerung* (Twilight of the Gods), when the gods are consumed by fire.

Traudl Junge, Hitler's youngest secretary, believed that Hanna was willing to die with her Führer. 'She adored Hitler', and 'sparkled with her fanatical, obsessive readiness to die for the Führer and his ideals'. But Hitler had other matters on his mind, issuing orders to non-existent battalions for a last-ditch defence of the capital and dictating his political testament to Junge, who hoped that she would now finally hear why the war had been necessary. Instead, 'her chief' trotted out the same old arguments and pretexts that now rang hollow in the claustrophobic and foetid concrete tomb under the Chancellery, the shattered symbol of the once indomitable Third Reich.

While Hanna waited for further orders, she busied herself between nursing Greim and entertaining the Goebbels' children with stories of her exploits. This caused her more pain than anything else, she would later admit, for their mother Magda had confided to Hanna that she and Dr Goebbels planned to kill all six of their children rather than let them live in a world without the Führer. She even asked Hanna if she would be willing to assist her if she lacked the strength to administer the fatal drugs when the time came.

Their equally deluded father saw their imminent suicide not as a tragic theatrical gesture but as glorious martyrdom and an 'eternal example' to all Germans 'that would long blaze as a holy thing from the pages of history'. Others shared in this mad vision as well as the hope that final victory might still be snatched from defeat at the eleventh hour. When the news came of President Roosevelt's death on 12 April, there was jubilation in the bunker and a surreal party atmosphere reigned, which was broken only days later when it became evident that the shelling was coming closer and the end was imminent.

Himmler's offer of surrender

On 27 April Hanna was summoned to Hitler's study and presented with two cyanide capsules, one for herself and the other for von Greim. In a faltering voice, Hitler told her that he and Eva Braun planned to commit suicide rather than risk having their bodies defiled after death as had been the fate of Mussolini and his mistress.

In the early hours of 29 April, Hitler appeared in von Greim's sick room clutching a telegram, his body shaking with rage, his face drained of colour. Himmler had betrayed him by contacting the Allies with an offer of surrender. This was the ultimate stab in the back for Hitler, who had considered Himmler his most loyal and trusted lieutenant. Greim was ordered to take a trainer monoplane that had managed to land nearby and liquidate Himmler. Then he was to organize a Luftwaffe attack on the advancing Russians with forces that had long been eradicated.

After making their hurried farewells and getting a perfunctory handshake from their Führer, Hanna and von Greim made their way back to the Victory Column where a pilot was waiting to fly them out of Berlin using the road near the Tiergarten in the middle of Berlin as a temporary landing strip.

Melitta's last flight

In mid-March, Melitta learned that her husband and the surviving adult members of his family had been transported to Buchenwald near Weimar, a concentration camp that was bursting at the seams with emaciated, brutalized prisoners. After using her name and reputation to acquire a visitor permit, she packed her Storch with food and linen and took off into an empty, clear spring sky, landing three hours later in a field close to the perimeter fence.

The sheer scale of the site took her breath away and the acrid stench of the smoke from the crematoria was sickening. Everywhere gaunt, haunted faces watched her as she presented her papers to the guards, then their eyes followed her while she unloaded the food and bedding and carried the items into the compound where her husband was being held. Although she had mentally prepared herself for this moment, her first sight of Alexander gave her a start. He looked as if he was just beginning to recover from a debilitating illness. The flesh had fallen away from his face so that he was all eyes and loosely sagging skin.

HER FIRST SIGHT OF ALEXANDER GAVE HER A START... THE FLESH HAD FALLEN AWAY FROM HIS FACE SO THAT HE WAS ALL EYES AND LOOSELY SAGGING SKIN

They exchanged news – she told him of what she knew of the other family members and of the military situation and he described in harrowing detail their imprisonment, interrogation and deportation. She managed to wave to the other family members in the distance before they were parted and she was ushered out of the compound and back to the waiting plane. Despite the danger of being shot down, Melitta made eight further visits to the camp but only managed to speak to her husband twice. On the other occasions, she delivered vital food and warm clothes, for which the prisoners named her the 'Flying Angel'.

Seven of the surviving Stauffenberg children were to have been taken from their children's home in Bad Sachsa to a concentration camp, but the train in which they were to be transported was forced to turn back when the railway station at nearby Nordhausen was hit in an Allied air raid. The children were then driven back to Bad Sachsa. It was a miraculous intervention for the children but their parents and other adult relatives were not so lucky.

Over the following days, Melitta attempted to follow the trail of Alexander and the other *Sippenhaft* prisoners (those condemned by association) as they were transported across Germany towards their final destination. At 7.20 on the morning of Sunday 8 April she was flying low along the Straubing-Passau railway line towards Schonberg in an unarmed Bücker Bü 181 when she was spotted by an American fighter on the prowl for troop and supply trains. The rear view of a Bücker looks remarkably similar to a Focke-Wulf Fw 190 and the American pilot evidently mistook Melitta's Bücker for the German fighter as he fired two short machine-gun bursts. Melitta managed to guide her plane to the ground, where she was helped out of the cockpit by a railway worker and a French POW, but she had been fatally wounded and died on the way to hospital. Despite her wounds, she had executed a textbook emergency landing unaware that only a few miles further south her husband and his fellow prisoners were en route to Dachau.

Lost war, lost family

Hanna's war ended in a civilian hospital in Kitzbühel, where she was attending to the badly injured von Greim. The pair had learned of Hitler's suicide and Germany's subsequent unconditional surrender during their long and arduous journey, but the final blow to Hanna's fading hopes was delivered when the Americans arrived and she was informed that her parents, her sister and her sister's three children were all dead. They had been shot by her father who feared the family would be repatriated to Hirschberg, which was now in the Soviet zone. He had then killed himself.

Hanna later wrote that she did not blame her father, who had taken upon himself 'the heaviest responsibility of all'. In her words, he was performing his 'overriding duty to preserve his family' by sparing them a life of suffering under Soviet occupation. It was a tragic act of self-preservation of a sort which only made sense in the chaos of post-war Germany. Having been conditioned to see themselves as invincible, the survivors could not accept the fact that they had been defeated by a superior force. In their eyes, they had merely been overrun by the indefatigable

Slavic hordes and their American allies, who had vastly larger resources at their disposal.

Hanna's belief in the Nazi worldview was unshaken by defeat. Like so many of her fellow countrymen and women, she refused to see Germany as the aggressor. In the ruins of the 'thousand-year Reich', the survivors cast themselves as the victims. They cited the destruction of Dresden, Hamburg and a dozen other cities as evidence of the Allies' indiscriminate 'over bombing' and the rape of their women by the Russians as indicative of the bestial nature of the Slavs. Such behaviour only confirmed their belief that the invasion of Russia and the subjugation of its 'racially inferior' inhabitants had been justified. Even after being confronted with the photographic and documentary evidence of the mass extermination of millions in the concentration and extermination camps, they stubbornly refused to believe such horrors had been perpetrated in their name and that the man they had put their faith in had instigated genocide on such a scale. The numbers were simply too fantastic to take in.

Holocaust denial

When Hanna was informally interrogated by the celebrated British test pilot Eric Brown, with whom she had been friendly during the pre-war years, she denied all knowledge of the camps. Brown had been to Belsen and had described the scene to her, but still she dismissed it as 'Allied propaganda'.

'She didn't want to believe any of it,' Brown later wrote. 'Nothing could convince her that the Holocaust took place.'

Even when faced with personal corroboration of such atrocities she still spoke of 'honour' among the Nazi leadership and only saw dishonour in those such as Goering and Himmler who had betrayed the regime and their Führer in a vain attempt to save their own skins.

In Brown's opinion she manipulated her interrogator, Captain Robert Work of the US Air Force Intelligence Unit, and 'made a fool out of him', exploiting the fact that she had never joined the Party to the point that he seriously considered employing her as an ambassador for reconciliation. But Work was no fool. He noted that she 'carefully weighs the "honour" aspect of every remark. The use of the word practically amounts to a fetish complex.' Honour and loyalty were all-too-convenient phrases that she trotted out to justify her lack of judgement and assuage her conscience.

> GREIM HAD COMMITTED SUICIDE BY BITING ON A CONCEALED CYANIDE CAPSULE... PROBABLY OUT OF FEAR OF BEING HANDED OVER TO THE RUSSIANS

When informed that von Greim had committed suicide by biting on a concealed cyanide capsule, she remarked that he must have done so because 'he could not reconcile his honour as a soldier with giving the information he would have had to give regarding the despicable traits and blunderings of Goering'. It is far more likely, however, that Greim's fear of being handed over to the Russians for interrogation was greater than any notion of betraying his own code of honour with regard to Goering.

Finding excuses for Hitler's psychopathy, she argued that his only crime was his failure to realize the incompetence of Goering. She laid the blame on the Führer's doctors who had prescribed so many drugs that he had developed a 'personality disorder' and 'was no longer responsible for his actions'. Although she conceded that Hitler had proved to be a disappointment as a military leader and statesman, she attributed his mental collapse to 'those who led him, lured him, criminally misdirected him, and informed him falsely'. Whether consciously or unconsciously, she could have been talking about herself and unconsciously creating a defence to excuse her own misguided loyalty.

A question of loyalty

Hanna's physical courage is unquestionable and her exploits are justly acknowledged, but self-interest and ambition led her to deny the criminal nature of the regime she so willingly served, even after she had been faced with the facts. To accept that she had been betrayed by the Führer she idolized would have taken more character than she evidently possessed.

She promised her captors that she would tell the truth about Hitler, 'the criminal incompetent', but when the Americans arranged a press conference she reneged on her promise and instead launched into an emotional rant in which she professed to have supported the regime and vowed she would do so again, if she had the chance.

During her captivity, she complained unceasingly about the conditions and the indignity of being incarcerated, the monotony of prison life and the lack of sympathy she believed she received from the guards, whom she imagined were mainly Jews. Writing to her brother from her cell, she said: 'We are delivered into the hands of the enemy [and] are at their mercy and, at that, of all their dirty methods.' But then she had never experienced the dread of being imprisoned by the Gestapo, as Melitta had.

At her own denazification hearing, she was able to present a number of highly favourable testimonials commonly known as *Persilscheine* (just like Persil the washing powder, *Persilscheine* washed a Nazi past clean) which described her in almost saintly terms, but the one statement which convinced the tribunal of her claim to be apolitical was the testimony of a Jewish pilot, Dr Joachim Kuttner. He had avoided transportation thanks to Hanna's efforts to find him work overseas in the mid-1930s, although she was not putting herself at risk by doing so at that time. Nevertheless, Kuttner felt he owed his life to Hanna and was happy to do what he could for her after the war.

However, when Hanna eventually came to write her memoirs after spending a little over a year in custody she took the opportunity to exonerate herself of all responsibility for supporting the regime and she denied all knowledge of its crimes. At the same time, her notion of loyalty demanded that she remained an unrepentant Nazi loyalist and apologist. As such she offered a highly selective version of the truth as she saw it, presenting a revisionist history of the Third Reich and casting herself as the ingenuous and apolitical heroine; an idealist and martyr for whom duty, honour and loyalty were paramount.

Melitta, too, had regarded loyalty as being among the chief virtues. Like Hanna, she was loyal to Germany, but unlike her rival she was loyal to the values of an older, traditional Germany, rather than to the ideals of a corrupt regime. Above all, though, she was loyal to the family into which she had married, risking her life time and again to take essential supplies and news from the outside world to them in Buchenwald and meeting a cruel fate in a last desperate attempt to reach her husband before he could be executed.

Melitta's physical courage was only one aspect of her remarkable personality. That was what distinguished Melitta von Stauffenberg from Hanna Reitsch.

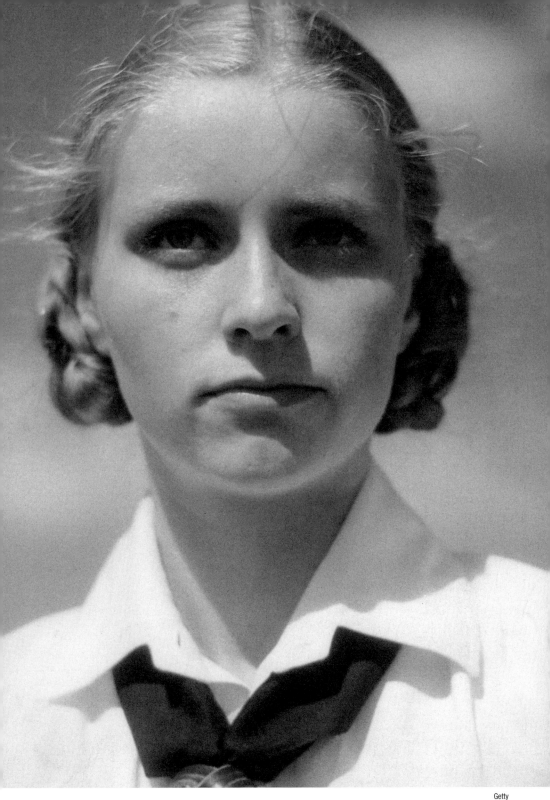

A BDM girl exemplifying the ideals of Nazi beauty photographed in 1937 by Max Ehlert, an official combat photographer for the Armed Forces Propaganda Company or PK. The *Bund Deutscher Mädel*, or League of German Girls, was the girls wing of the Hitler Youth and its members were indoctrinated with Nazi values designed to make them dutiful wives, mothers and home-makers.

It's 1934, and a young mother enjoys the attention as she wheels her two young children through Berlin in a pram decorated with swastikas. In 1871, German archaeologist Heinrich Schliemann discovered swastika-like decorations on pottery on what was thought to be the site of ancient Troy. The swastika soon became a good luck sign throughout the western world, but right-wing Germans, bidding to create a new national identity for the 20th century, adapted it for their own purposes as the symbol of the Nazis – a fascist version of the hammer and sickle. The swastika was widely featured in propaganda photographs and posters for the Third Reich, and it is still used to intimidate today.

As part of the Nazis' pageant of power, a class of young girls performs the Hitler salute for the camera (in 1940) as a battalion of SA stormtroopers goosesteps by. A key part of the spectacle, women and girls were expected to adopt traditional German peasant costumes, with their hair in plaits or buns and flat shoes. Make-up and trousers were frowned upon, as were dyed hair and smoking in public. The Nazis largely removed women from the positions of power they had enjoyed in the Weimar Republic, but Propaganda MInister Joseph Goebbels didn't admit to any such thing. Instead he declared: 'The mission of women is to be beautiful and to bring children into the world.'

The lavish society wedding in Munich in 1937 of Marianne Schönmann, daughter of opera singer Maria Petzl, with its guest list of inner-circle Nazis. Eva Braun is fourth from the left in the second row, while her sister Gretl kneels on the floor to the right of the happy couple. Adolf Hitler looks ill at ease immediately behind her. The gathering includes Hitler's photographer Heinrich Hoffmann (the portly man, extreme left), Hitler's physician Theo Morrell (his face partially obscured in front of the painting) and illusionist Helmut Schreiber (to the left of Hitler, whom he often advised).

Three of the famous Mitford Sisters in 1932, (l to r) Unity, Diana and Nancy. Diana married Oswald Mosley the English fascist leader, and she and Unity went to the Nuremberg Rally of 1933 as part of the delegation of the British Union of Fascists. After hearing him speak, Unity 'worshipped' Hitler and, after 'stalking' him in Munich, gained access to 'the greatest man of all time', as she described him. Once Britain and Germany went to war in 1939, she took a pearl-handled pistol given to her by Hitler for protection, and shot herself in the head. She returned to Britain to convalesce in 1940 and, eight years later, died of meningitis caused by the bullet still lodged in her head.

Paula Hitler after her arrest by US troops in May 1945: she later returned to Vienna where she worked in an arts and crafts shop. Paula was the youngest sister of Adolf, but used the surname Hiedler (the original spelling of 'Hitler'). She only met Eva Braun once. When she died in 1960, she was the only remaining member of Adolf Hitler's family.

Gertrud Scholtz-Klink, the leader of the Nazi Women's League, was known as the female Führer. Despite the vaulting ambition of her own career, she insisted that women should never be involved in politics and constantly promoted the idea that a woman's place was in the home producing children. She had 11 herself. Presumed dead at the time of the Nuremberg Trials, she and her husband were discovered living in Bebenhausen, near Tübingen, by the Americans a couple of years later, and imprisoned. She remained an unrepentant Nazi to the end of her days.

Just five feet tall, Hanna Reitsch became the top German female pilot of her day. Aged 21, she set a new world altitude record for unpowered flight in a glider, and moved on to test-fly such models as the jet-powered ME262 as well as the prototype manned V-1 rocket. As a colleague put it, Reitsch was 'a symbol of German womanhood and the idol of German aviation'. She was also a devoted admirer of Adolf Hitler; in fact, she begged to be allowed to die with him in the Führerbunker at the end of World War II. In the event, she flew the last plane out of Berlin, taking off from an improvised airstrip in the Tiergarten as the Red Army marched in. Later she said: 'Many Germans feel guilty about the war. But they don't explain the real guilt we share – the fact that we lost.'

Melitta Schenk Gräfin von Stauffenberg, was a rival of Reitsch. Like her, she was awarded the title of *Flugkapitän* as well as the Iron Cross – in her case for performing over 1,500 test flights in dive bombers (in total, she flew over 2,500). A talented designer, she introduced many innovations in night-flight technology and pushed herself to the limit to test them. In 1944, she was arrested along with other members of the Stauffenberg family for conspiring to murder Hitler, but she was released. Melitta was half-Jewish and a German patriot but could never be called a Nazi; she felt it was her duty to do everything she could to help those who served in the Luftwaffe, but was tormented by the idea of helping Hitler. In 1945, she died after being shot down by an Allied fighter plane.

1933, and this is the first married couple to enjoy the credit scheme introduced by Hitler's government to encourage women to stop working. 'Aryan' newlyweds were eligible for an interest-free loan of 1,000 Reichsmarks in the form of household vouchers made out in the husband's name. Repayments could be lowered by having children, which led to a 'baby boom'. The idea had been to free up jobs for men, but by 1937 full employment (for men) was achieved and women were once more needed in the workplace.

Violette Morris was a gifted athlete who excelled at the shot put and discus and who played football for Olympique de Paris from 1920 to 1926. Despite her athletic activities, Morris smoked heavily and swore like a trouper. She was refused a licence by the French Women's Athletic Federation over her bisexual lifestyle and banned from the 1928 Olympics. She can be seen in court (left) suing the federation in 1930. In 1935, she was recruited into the SD, the Nazi security service, at the personal request of Adolf Hitler and the information she gave the Germans was crucial for the invasion of France. In 1944, she was killed by the French resistance and buried in a communal grave.

A woman from the Saarland walks a dog with a balloon attached to its collar, saying: 'The Saar is German.' The Treaty of Versailles had left the Saar under the control of the League of Nations for 15 years. A plebiscite was held. The vote was by no means a foregone conclusion since many anti-Nazis had fled to the Saar after 1933. But helped by the Saar police and the Gestapo, the Nazis boycotted, intimidated and beat their way to victory. On 13 January 1935, the plebiscite took place; the result was overwhelming: 90.3% of the voters voted to return to Germany, or so the Nazis claimed.

CHAPTER FIVE

Hitler's Jewish Princess

Stephany Julienne Richter acquired the Austrian title of Princess Hohenlohe-Waldenburg-Schillingsfürst through marriage. A title she retained after her divorce not many years later.

Not only was she a princess but she also radiated personality and charm, a heady mix that few men could resist, even the Führer. He was so smitten with her that he totally overlooked the fact that she was a Jew and invited her to visit the Reich Chancellery on many occasions. She even claimed that they were intimate.

As well as acting as a glamorous hostess for the Nazi regime, she also undertook a number of missions for Hitler, several of them to Britain. Lord Rothermere, the press baron, was one of her prime targets. All of this brought her rich rewards.

Her charmed existence came to an end when first Hitler and then Lord Rothermere dropped her. Then after moving to the US, she was arrested by the FBI in 1941 and interned until the end of the war. However, once hostilities ended she once again fascinated and seduced all those around her, right up to her death in 1972.

On 30 January 1938 *Time* magazine carried a story that piqued the interest of American isolationists and anti-fascists alike.

> Titian-haired, 40-year-old Stephanie Juliana Princess Hohenlohe-Waldenburg-Schillingsfürst, confidante of the Führer and friend of half of Europe's great, is scheduled to sail from England to the US this week. Since the fall of Austria, Princess Stephanie, once the toast of Vienna, has lent her charms to advancing the Nazi cause in circles where it would do the most good.

The Austrian-born aristocrat was for a time a high-profile pawn in the diplomatic game of bluff and brinkmanship that Hitler was playing out on the eve of the war he had always wanted. But behind the scenes the high society beauty was more than an unofficial intermediary and glamorous hostess – much more. In her unpublished memoirs, Princess Stephanie claimed to be intimate with Hitler and wrote that he was infatuated with her, to the consternation of his mistress Eva Braun, a fact that is all the more remarkable given that she was Jewish – and Hitler knew it.

Ernst Hanfstaengl, an influential friend and confidant of the Führer, warned the dictator that he was compromising himself with a 'full-bloodied Jewess' and an alleged 'black-mailer'. To placate Hanfstaengl, Hitler ordered the Gestapo to look into her family history and was subsequently assured that the allegations were unfounded, according to the official report. However, this was not in fact the case. Princess

Stephanie's mother, Ludmilla Kuranda, was indeed a Czech Jew and according to the princess's half-sister, Gina Kaus, her real father was Max Wiener, a Jewish money-lender with whom her mother had a lengthy affair. But the princess was too valuable to the regime and so Himmler had her declared 'an honorary Aryan'.

However, Hitler's inner circle resented Princess Stephanie's pernicious influence for reasons other than her racial origins, for she had cultivated a reputation as an adventuress and manipulative intriguer whose motivations were never clear. Money was certainly not an incentive. She was one of the wealthiest women in Europe, having married and divorced Prince Friedrich Franz von Hohenlohe-Waldenburg-Schillingsfürst, from whom she received a generous settlement as well as her title. She had prevailed upon him to marry her by claiming that she was pregnant with their child when, in fact, the father was another of her lovers, the Italian Archduke Franz Salvator, son-in-law to the Austrian Emperor Franz Joseph I.

Meeting Hitler

Motherhood and domesticity held no attraction for her and when war broke out in 1914 she volunteered to serve as a nurse on the Eastern Front, although she must have been the only nurse to be accompanied by her servants. To her credit, she ditched her retinue when she went with the Austrian army to Italy and she remained in uniform until the end of the war.

In the years preceding her fateful meeting with Hitler, she seduced a succession of wealthy lovers and was said to have made all of them pay richly for the privilege. She was determined to make an equally striking and memorable impression on the Nazi leader.

In December 1933, she prevailed upon her then lover, Captain Fritz Wiedemann, Hitler's personal adjutant and his former commanding officer in the Great War, to effect the introduction. Taking great pains to choose a dress that she thought would appeal to him and affecting her most aristocratic pose she charmed him from the first. He received her with uncharacteristic affection, taking her hand in his and kissing it, to the astonishment of his other guests. Although he was known to be distrustful of intelligent women and intellectuals in general, he appeared to be impressed with the princess, who spoke several languages fluently and was well versed in current affairs, something at which the Nazi foreign minister, von Ribbentrop, was proving inept.

Hitler, who disapproved of smoking, was not then aware of her habit of smoking cigars in company or her decidedly unladylike manner of lighting them by striking the match on the heel of her shoe. An invitation to take tea with Hitler in private followed that first official meeting, during which she claimed that they sat side by side and he could not take his eyes off her the entire time.

She later confided in her unpublished memoirs that:

> He hardly ever smiles, except when making a sarcastic remark. He can be, he often is, very bitter. I think I can truthfully say that with the exception of his very intimate circle I am one of the few persons with whom he held normal conversations. By that I mean one where both parties speak in turn: a conversation of two human beings. Usually this is not the case. He either makes a speech and one has to listen, or else he sits there with a dead serious face, never opening his mouth.

She quickly became a regular guest at private screenings of his favourite films – romantic musicals and sentimental melodramas – during which he would stroke her hair and caress her cheek. It was all innocent enough, or so it seemed, but there were rumours that Hitler's attraction to her was becoming an embarrassment to his closest advisers and would be potentially disastrous to his authority if the relationship became public.

Rivals for Hitler's attention

In their own way the Mitford sisters, apart from the conventional Deborah, were no less colourful than Princess Stephanie. Diana Mitford had left her husband for Oswald Mosley, the founder of the British Union of Fascists, Jessica was a communist and Unity was devoted to the Nazi cause. When Unity and Jessica shared a bedroom, they drew a chalk line down the middle. On Jessica's side were pictures of Lenin and hammer and sickle images while on Unity's side were displayed pictures of Hitler, with swastikas everywhere. Perhaps Unity, who always felt herself to be in competition with her sisters, had first turned to Nazism as a way of giving herself the notoriety and glamour she craved.

Unfortunately, things did not stop there. Unity became fatally attracted to Hitler and was rumoured to be insanely jealous of his association with Princess Stephanie. On one occasion, she became so incensed that she ranted at Hitler: 'Here you are, an anti-Semite, and yet you have a Jewish woman, Princess Hohenlohe, around you all the time.' Hitler simply ignored her. That occasion was the 1935 Nuremberg Party Rally, which the princess had described as an 'orgy of dedication to the Nazi creed'.

Mitford was also envious of the way in which Hitler took her rival into his confidence with regard to relations with 'Germany's friends', especially those within the British establishment. In her unpublished memoirs, the princess confided:

> Every visit of mine to the Reich Chancellery seemed to them an impudent encroachment upon their sacred privileges, and every hour that Adolf wasted upon me was an hour which he might have spent to so much greater advantage in their devoted company.

Predictably the British intelligence services were monitoring Princess Stephanie's activities and in a report dating from

1938 they observed: 'She is frequently summoned by the Führer who appreciates her intelligence and good advice. She is perhaps the only woman who can exercise any influence on him.'

She was a shrewd judge of character and saw how masterfully Hitler manipulated those in his thrall.

> In 1938 during the September crisis Hitler sent for Unity Mitford. When she arrived, he told her that in view of the gravity of the situation he wanted her to leave Germany. Though it would seem that such a gesture was prompted only by friendly concern towards one of his most ardent admirers, his intention was of a different nature. His real purpose in sending for Unity Mitford was to make her return to England and impress her people and all those she would naturally talk to with the gravity of the situation. This is an example of his cunning and supreme ability to make use of even the slightest incident. He is a master at the understanding of, and playing upon, the psychology of people, which I consider his greatest gift and asset.

Her racial origins made it extremely unlikely that she was a true believer in National Socialism and yet she volunteered to act as an unpaid emissary for the regime. She was even accused of being a Nazi spy by several European newspapers, although she was not arrested or questioned at the time. However, the release of declassified files in 2005 unearthed a secret MI6 report dating from 1933 which detailed payments totalling £300,000 (equal to £13 million today) to be made to her in the event that she succeeded in convincing British newspaper magnate

> STEPHANIE WAS ACCUSED OF BEING A NAZI SPY BY SEVERAL EUROPEAN PAPERS, ALTHOUGH SHE WASN'T ARRESTED OR QUESTIONED AT THE TIME

Lord Rothermere to campaign for the return to Germany of territory annexed by Poland in 1919.

Princess Stephanie dutifully courted Rothermere in the casinos of Monte Carlo, where they both gambled recklessly for high stakes. If she didn't win at roulette, she at least succeeded in making him a fervent convert to the National Socialist cause.

The princess and the publisher

In September 1930, following the Nazi Party's triumph in the national elections, Lord Rothermere accepted an invitation from Hitler to visit Munich, the crucible of National Socialism. The Nazis were then the second-largest party in the Reichstag and the publisher was keen to put his newspapers and considerable influence at Hitler's disposal. The subsequent article was a substantial boost to the appeasement movement, who now saw the Nazis as the only defence against communism.

In return for acting as an intermediary between the press baron and the dictator, Princess Stephanie found herself rewarded by both parties. The tycoon put her on the payroll to the tune of £5,000 per annum (around £200,000/$270,000 today), which must have assuaged her anger when she read the first of his rabidly anti-Semitic editorials in the *Daily Mail*. These appeared with increasing ferocity, culminating in the most inflammatory and offensive piece on 10 July 1933, in which he condemned his rivals for printing stories 'obsessed' with Nazi racist violence and praised Hitler for suppressing an imaginary global Jewish conspiracy (which he described as 'Israelites of international attachments').

Rothermere had one of these diatribes affixed to a photographic self-portrait and mounted in a solid gold frame, which was to be presented in person by the princess as a gift to Hitler. But when Jewish-owned businesses threatened to withdraw their advertising, Rothermere abandoned his principles overnight and also withdrew his support for Oswald Mosley's extremist nationalist party, the British Union of Fascists.

To further their own ends and establish the princess as their unofficial ambassador, the Nazis funded her lavish lifestyle to the tune of 20,000 Reichsmarks and authorized Hitler's adjutant Captain Wiedemann to buy her expensive clothes and other luxury goods to keep her sweet. Wiedemann subsequently accompanied her to the United States in November 1937, where she whipped up support among the pro-Nazi German-American Bund.

In 1939 Hermann Goering set her up in Schloss Leopoldskron, the magnificent and recently restored rococo palace in Salzburg which the Nazis had seized from theatre director and émigré Max Reinhardt. The castle was to serve as a luxury hotel for VIPs visiting the Berghof, Hitler's Alpine retreat on the Obersalzberg, near Berchtesgaden, Bavaria, which was a 40-minute drive away. Princess Stephanie was in her element and relished the role of hostess, wining and dining a succession of foreign diplomats and dignitaries who were to be softened up before being presented with the dictator's latest territorial demands.

Mission to London

As *Time* magazine reported on 30 January 1938:

> During the Czecho-Slovak crisis she did yeoman service for the Nazi campaign. When Mr. Chamberlain sent Lord Runciman to gather impressions of conditions in Czechoslovakia Princess Stephanie hurried to the Sudetenland castle of Prince Max Hohenlohe where the British mediator was entertained.

But by the following month Hitler's hostess was entertaining something entirely different – second thoughts regarding the nature of the regime to which she had lent her name. She wrote to Lord Rothermere, warning him to be less vociferous in his support for what she had finally come to see as an administration composed entirely of 'extremists'.

> You must be very careful in future. I do not see how it will be possible for you, under these new conditions, to continue to support Hitler in future and at the same time serve the interests of your own country.

But if she was finally questioning her commitment to a warmongering tyrant, she did not betray her true feelings to her German friends, who honoured her with the Gold Medal of the Nazi Party on 10 June, in a ceremony presided over by Hitler himself.

The Nazis were very generous with other people's property, buying loyalty with stolen loot for which they expected much in return. That gold medal too came at a price. The princess was entrusted with a delicate mission and one that could determine the course of the coming war.

She was instructed to travel to London to enquire into the possibility of a public visit to Britain by Reichsmarschall Goering, with a view to conducting unofficial talks between the Nazi administration and the British government. The Germans were eager to avoid provoking a war with Britain in the coming months, when the Wehrmacht were to march across the borders of its European neighbours. The princess was to enlist the help of her friend Lady Snowdon in setting up a meeting with Lord Halifax, the British foreign secretary, to see if it might be possible for Goering to, in the words of Lord Halifax, 'come to England without being too severely and publicly insulted, and what attitude H.M. Government would take generally to such a visit'.

Hitler's ardour cools

As keen as Prime Minister Neville Chamberlain might have been to avoid another European war, his government were not prepared to entertain Reichsmarschall Goering in Whitehall, or anywhere else for that matter. And as for Princess Stephanie, her approach and her credibility were regarded within diplomatic circles as highly suspect. Halifax had been informed by Walford Selby, the British ambassador to Vienna, that she was a Nazi agent and that her suite at the Dorchester hotel was an 'outpost of German espionage'. MI6 had been told by French intelligence, the Deuxième Bureau, that there was strong evidence to suggest that she was a spy, a conclusion confirmed by MI5, although MI5's source appears to have been a dubious one – Princess Stephanie's maid, Anna Stoffl.

A more reliable source was the German journalist Bella Fromm, who accused the princess of being: 'One of the most fanatical exponents of National Socialist ideology ... She was one of the first female agents sent abroad by the Nazis before they came to power.'

Wiedemann, for his part, gave the princess credit for 'straightening relations' between Britain and Germany during the Munich crisis of September 1938. In a letter to Lord Rothermere shortly after Neville Chamberlain had submitted to Hitler's demands and signed over the fate of Czechoslovakia, Wiedemann conceded: 'It was her ground-work which made the Munich agreement possible.'

If she harboured doubts about serving Hitler, a man who tore up treaties as readily as he demolished Viennese pastries or cream cakes, she kept it under her immaculately coiffured Titian hair and in public at least continued to be an effusive advocate of the regime. After Chamberlain had signed the Munich Treaty – which allowed the Nazis to annex the Sudetenland, a region of Czechoslovakia that was predominantly populated by ethnic Germans – she wrote to Hitler praising his diplomacy:

There are moments in life that are so great – I mean, where one feels so deeply that it is almost impossible to find the right words to express one's feelings – Herr Reich Chancellor, please believe me that I have shared with you the experience and emotion of every phase of the events of the last weeks. What none of your subjects in their wildest dreams dared hope for – you have made come true. That must be the finest thing a head of state can give to himself and to his people. I congratulate you with all my heart.

However, Hitler's ardour cooled on learning that Wiedemann was Stephanie's lover. It is remarkable that the pair had managed to keep their relationship a secret from the Führer for so long, but once Hitler's informants had confirmed the rumours, he saw his pocket princess as soiled goods. Wiedemann was given an ultimatum – accept a reassignment to the German Embassy in San Francisco, or face the consequences of displeasing his Führer. He accepted the 'promotion' and a generous salary for making the right decision but he continued to hanker after his lover, who had taken the hint that her presence was no longer required at the Berghof and had relocated to London.

There she experienced her second rebuff when Lord Rothermere informed her that he was terminating their agreement in the light of her loss of influence with Hitler. Incensed, she threatened to sue him for breach of contract. He called her bluff and lived to regret it, because she made public the full extent of the British newspaper magnate's cosy relationship with the regime.

The end of the road

When the case was over she left for the United States to be reunited with her lover, but she was now under surveillance by the FBI for her active incitement of anti-democratic forces within the country. Bureau chief J. Edgar Hoover took a personal interest in a woman he described as being 'extremely intelligent, dangerous and cunning' and who was:

worse than 10,000 men ... I would like to stress emphatically that in my opinion this woman's visa ought not to be renewed. I would further suggest that she be deported from the United States at the earliest possible moment.

But it was not until 8 December 1941, following the Japanese attack on Pearl Harbor and Hitler's impulsive declaration of war against the US that day, that she was arrested and interned at a facility in Philadelphia, and then at a camp for enemy aliens in Texas, as a 'potential danger to public security and peace', along with her son Prince Franz Hohenlohe. She remained in custody, enjoying 'special privileges', until May 1945, when Germany surrendered. After the war she continued to attract wealthy male lovers and was feted by Long Island society, to the annoyance of some, who thought she merited a worse fate. She returned to Germany in 1959, where her unrivalled access to the drawing-rooms of the world brought her well-paid contracts with leading magazine publishers. She continued to be a subject of newspaper gossip columns until her death in Geneva in June 1972.

Her obituary had effectively been written more than thirty years earlier when the *New York Times* summed up her contribution to the Third Reich.

The princess is without doubt the star among a whole group of female members of the former German aristocracy who had been recruited by Hitler for a wide variety of operations, many of a secret nature. They have been acting as political spies, propaganda hostesses, social butterflies and ladies of mystery ... On orders from the Nazi Party, Princess Hohenlohe has placed the heads of Lords, Counts, and other highly placed personages at the feet of Hitler.

CHAPTER SIX

Adolf's Eyes and Ears – Spying for Hitler

When it came to spying, Hitler managed to overcome his aversion to employing women in responsible roles, because it was often much easier for a woman, particularly an attractive one, to gain access to sensitive areas.

Women took to espionage and sometimes the betrayal of their own kind for a number of reasons. Some felt that they had been badly treated by their own countries or were escaping a possible death sentence. Others might just have been motivated by the authority and privileges that came with being a traitor.

However, it is more difficult to see what motivated an ordinary-sounding US girl to transmit vile propaganda on behalf of her Nazi masters. The only reason seems to be that she was escaping her dead-end life back in the US.

But perhaps no one could be more treacherous than the girl who betrayed her own people.

Adolf Hitler had declared that National Socialism would be 'an exclusively male revolution' and was openly contemptuous of women in uniform. He admonished Hitler Youth leader Baldur von Schirach for allowing members of the BDM to march in parade at the 1932 Nuremberg Rally, but had no reservations regarding the recruitment of women to spy for the regime, even though doing so would have resulted in them being executed had they been captured by the Allies.

Nazi agents were conspicuously inept, with many being arrested before they could complete their mission and so few have merited more than a footnote in the standard histories of the Second World War.

Lilly Stein

Lilly Stein was an exception. The Austrian-born brunette was recruited by the Abwehr (German Military Intelligence Service) in 1938 primarily on account of her social connections. A wealthy socialite, she was said to have used her close relationship with American diplomat and US State Department official Ogden H. Hammond, Jr. to establish a high-class fashion house in New York in 1939, which served as a front for a Nazi spy ring. It was nominally led by Frederick 'Fritz' Duquesne, a South African, but it was Lilly who recruited agents from among the disaffected German population and who forwarded their messages and stolen documents to Berlin on microfilm and it was she who issued their instructions.

She was conscientious and careful, refusing to put anything incriminating in writing, but her associates were not so discreet and her superiors made the fatal mistake of abusing her trust. Payments were late and often far below what she had expected for the quality of the information she sold them and for the risks she took in obtaining it. She complained that she was forced to find employment as an artist's model to supplement her income and eventually she had to close the shop due to lack of funds.

The ring was ultimately betrayed by William Sebold, a naturalized American citizen who had only agreed to spy for his Fatherland out of fear for what might happen to his family back in Germany. He was in fact a double agent and had handed over his codebook to the FBI, who used it to transmit misinformation to Berlin.

FRENCH ATHLETE VIOLETTE MORRIS TURNED TRAITOR AFTER HER CAREER WAS CUT SHORT BY THE WOMEN'S NATIONAL SPORTS FEDERATION

After the Japanese attack on Pearl Harbor on 7 December 1941, Germany too declared war on the United States in support of its Axis ally and American Nazi sympathizers were rounded up and interred as enemy aliens. All 33 members of the Duquesne ring were arrested and indicted for treason, with only Sebold escaping. When they were tried, all of them were convicted. Lilly Stein asserted that she had been coerced into spying when the Nazis annexed Austria in March 1938 but her plea for leniency fell on deaf ears and she was sentenced to ten years in prison.

Violette Morris

The women who spied for Hitler did so for different reasons. Many of them were zealous converts to National Socialism while others were motivated by fear of what might happen to them or their families if they refused. Some were simply driven by a lust for revenge against those whom they believed had betrayed them.

French athlete Violette Morris turned traitor after her career was cut short by the women's national sports federation, the FFSF (Fédération française sportive féminine). Its officials revoked her licence and prohibited her from participating in the 1928 Summer Olympic Games, citing as a reason Violette's unfeminine attire, specifically her habit of wearing trousers, but also objecting to her 'undignified' habit of chain smoking, swearing like a sailor and physically assaulting any referees whose decisions she disagreed with. There were also allegations that she handed out amphetamines to her teammates.

She was proud of her 'butch' lesbian image and flouted her sexuality in public, visiting Paris night clubs dressed in a three-piece suit and tie.

The German press were fascinated by the 5ft 5in juggernaut with 14-inch biceps who had won gold medals for throwing the javelin and putting the shot in the 1921 and 1922 Women's World Games in Monte Carlo. She excelled at several sports. She was no slouch at swimming and was also a celebrated prize fighter, flattening all comers in the boxing ring. But she was equally fearless behind the wheel of a racing car, having served as a courier and ambulance driver in the Great War at Verdun. When she was banned from racing, she lost her means of earning a living and used her loss of earnings to sue the FFSF. She also resorted to having her breasts surgically removed, so that she could sit more comfortably in the driving seat.

However, her case against the sports federation was undermined by her insistence on wearing trousers, which was explicitly forbidden by French law (a law that was only repealed in 2013). Her dispute with the FFSF went to trial in 1930 and though she employed the services of the eminent lawyer Maître Lot the verdict went against her. She used the proceedings to publicize her loathing for what she believed to be the endemic corruption in French politics and public life.

We live in a country rotten by money and scandals, governed by phrases, scoundrels and trouble-makers. This country of small people is not worthy of its elders, not worthy to survive. One day its decadence will lead him to the rank of a slave. But I, if I am still there, I will not be one of the slaves. Believe me. That's not in my temperament.

Recruited by the Nazis

It was then that she met a former racing rival, Gertrude Hannecker, now a journalist, who recruited her to work for the SD, the SS Security Service. They exploited her personal contacts and her mobility, which enabled her to scout out French military defences and record the deployment of troops and tanks. Her previous war experience proved invaluable in that respect and the fact that she now owned a car repair business meant that she had both vehicles and unlimited fuel, as well as a legitimate reason for driving around the country without arousing suspicion. Among her celebrity friends was the avant-garde poet and filmmaker Jean Cocteau, who cajoled Violette into driving him to the front line during the 'phoney war' of September 1939, so he could visit his male lover who had enlisted in the army.

It was perhaps as much for her image as for her athletic achievements that she was feted by the Nazis, who invited her to attend the 1936 Berlin Olympics as a personal guest of the Führer. Is it possible that Hitler was attracted to her because of his habit of surrounding himself with people who were either physically challenged in some way or did not conform to the norms of society? For instance, Goebbels, his propaganda minister, had a club foot and a short, polio-weakened body. And Himmler, short-sighted and physically weak, exhibited none of the physical qualities that he demanded from his SS recruits. Homosexuality, too, was rife in Nazi circles, in spite of the Nazis' persecution of such people. For instance, Hitler's closest friend, Ernst Roehm, leader of the SA, was openly homosexual (as were many in the SA). Hitler perhaps realized that disaffected waifs and strays had more to lose and so were easier to manipulate.

Whatever Hitler's reasons for feting Violette, her reports on the movements of the French troops, including their deployment of armour, proved a significant factor in the rout of the French army in June 1940. After the fall of France, she was employed as a driver for the German officers and their Vichy collaborators and also became involved in the distribution of black market goods, but it is said that she then took a more active role by serving the French Gestapo, the Carlingue. She was accused of participating in the interrogation and torture of prisoners in the Rue Lauriston, which earned her the nickname 'The Hyena'.

As a consequence, her name was added to a long list of Nazi agents who were to be liquidated on the eve of D-Day. She had also been targeted because of her part in thwarting the missions carried out by the SOE (Special Operations Executive), the British-sponsored sabotage and reconnaissance unit, in cooperation with the French resistance.

On 26 April 1944, the Maquis (French resistance fighters) ambushed the car she was travelling in and machine-gunned the occupants. Violette was killed along with her friends and their two children.

Marina Lee

On the whole, Hitler's female spies were far more effective than their male counterparts. Former Russian ballerina Marina Lee may have been the most successful of all. It is thought that she abandoned communism and fled to Norway, using a Swedish passport, because her parents were believed to have been murdered by the Bolsheviks. She then married a Norwegian.

In 1940 Marina, who was described as 'blond, tall, with a beautiful figure, refined and languid in manner' and reportedly fluent in five languages, used her undoubted charm to inveigle herself into General Auchinleck's headquarters at Tromsø and steal the British Navy's plans for the invasion of Norway, thus enabling the Germans to stave off certain defeat.

According to a captured German agent, Gerth van Wijk, her information forewarned General Eduard Dietl of the British plans, so that he was able to reorganize the coastal defences in time to push the British and their French allies back to the sea, leaving behind men and equipment they could ill afford to lose at this early stage in the war. Norwegian troops who had risked their lives to support the invasion then found themselves cut adrift by their retreating allies.

Dietl had been close to withdrawing his men from the strategically significant port of Narvik and surrendering when he was informed of the British strategy and shown their plan. The invasion could have marked a significant reversal for the Germans that early in the war, as strategic resources would have been denied to them by the Allied presence. The Norwegian resistance would also have been encouraged to retaliate against the German occupying forces and the Allies would have had a base from which to launch an offensive against Germany from the north.

The defeat was a humiliating set-back for the British, though it could be said that Marina's daring coup was ultimately counterproductive as it saw Conservative prime minister Neville Chamberlain resign only to be replaced by Winston Churchill, whose galvanizing speeches and vigorous leadership sustained British morale during the darker days of the war.

Marina was last seen in Spain, where she had continued working for the Abwehr.

Axis Sally

'This is Berlin calling. Berlin calling the American mothers, wives and sweethearts. And I'd just like to say, girls, when Berlin calls it pays to listen.'

Her velvet tone was intended to sound like every GI's big sister or favourite aunt, but Mildred Gillars, aka Axis Sally, became 'the voice you love to hate'. During the war, her daily propaganda broadcast from the heart of Nazi Germany was listened to with a mixture of derision and consternation by American forces serving overseas, and their families back home, as she listed the latest casualties with barely suppressed glee. Many found her perversely entertaining, particularly the troops who tuned in to while away the long tedious hours they spent off-duty. They jeered at her obvious attempts to demoralize them. Their families knew they shouldn't listen, but they were seduced by her homely Midwest accent and the disconcerting fact that she was able to name the wounded, the dead and those who had been taken prisoner, even giving their hometowns.

She preyed on their fears, cruelly teasing them to expect more deaths by the day and getting under the skin of even the most patriotic by questioning why they were sacrificing their sons, fathers and brothers 'for Franklin D. Roosevelt and Churchill and their Jewish cohorts'. She also relished the role of the vindictive snoop, urging GIs to question their sweetheart's fidelity. 'Who is going out with your girl while you're fighting a long way from home?' she would ask in a snide and spiteful tone.

Fitting the profile

'Midge', to use her official German radio name, fitted the profile of the bitter and twisted propagandist. That is, she was a mediocrity and an opportunist who cynically exploited a catastrophe to make a name for herself. She was a born fantasist and a frustrated actress who had flunked college then failed to find work in New York after leaving home to escape her mother and her stepfather, who she claimed was an alcoholic. After taking a series of dead-end, poorly-paid jobs she finally emigrated to Germany in 1934, where she found work as a radio presenter.

> **MILDRED GILLARS WAS A BORN FANTASIST AND FRUSTRATED ACTRESS WHO HAD FLUNKED COLLEGE, THEN FAILED TO FIND WORK IN NEW YORK AFTER LEAVING HOME**

Mildred was feted by a regime keen to recruit native English speakers who shared its abhorrence for the American way of life. She was able to spew out her virulent anti-Semitism and be commended, rather than censured, for it. 'I'd rather die for Germany than live for one hundred years on milk and honey in the Jewish America of today,' she whined, to the evident satisfaction of her Nazi bosses. And she was amply rewarded for her treachery, enjoying a generous salary, a certain celebrity and all the luxuries denied her stateside sisters.

Her fantasy ended with the fall of the Nazi regime when she was shipped back to the United States to stand trial for treason, although she was not the only American citizen who had broadcast enemy propaganda. A namesake of hers had operated in Italy. Mildred served 12 years in prison before being released on parole in 1961.

She died in 1988 and is buried in an unmarked grave in Columbus, Ohio, near the convent in which she sought anonymity and seclusion for the rest of her life.

Stella Goldschlag - the blonde ghost

There is surely no more contemptible person than one who betrays their own people. And though none of us knows for certain how we would respond if we were forced to choose between certain death and betraying our friends, we would all like to believe that we would have the courage to resist and somehow survive.

But not everyone has the spirit and selflessness of a Schindler or a Wallenberg. Tragically, many Jews reluctantly cooperated with their Nazi oppressors in the mistaken belief that they or their families might be spared transportation to the camps. Others assisted in the round-ups of Jews as members of the Judenrat (Jewish Council) or the Jewish police because they naively believed that the Nazis would resettle them, disregarding rumours that they would be sent to their deaths. A few may even have relished the opportunity to exercise power over their former neighbours and settle petty personal scores. Sadly, Jews were not immune from the failings and defects that afflicted their persecutors.

Pretty Berliner Stella Goldschlag was, however, one of a kind. If those who knew her are to be believed, the tall, curvaceous blue-eyed blonde was an unprincipled, pathological liar who bitterly resented her Jewish heritage. In return for an assurance that she and her parents would be spared transportation, she agreed to entice the untergetaucht or 'submerged' Jews out of hiding – those who lived among the population using false identity papers and who refused to wear the oblig-atory yellow star – by callously exploiting her glamorous movie star figure and looks. There were an estimated 18,300 'U-Boats' living in Berlin and the Gestapo were determined to root them out.

She was so successful that she was soon put on the Gestapo payroll, receiving a generous reward for ensnaring her fellow Jews and earning herself the nickname 'Blonde Poison' among those she had betrayed.

The source of her inverted anti-Semitism is not known. She was by all accounts a precocious, pampered child born to indulgent, middle-class parents. Her father earned a good living as a newsreel editor and her mother was well paid as a singer. They lived comfortably in a small apart-ment on Xantner Strasse in Wilmersdorf, an affluent district of Berlin whose residents had included Berthold Brecht and Marlene Dietrich. Both celebrities, however, had emigrated during the mass exodus of artists and intellectuals in 1933. The Goldschlags were not tempted to follow, having heard that the emigration process for ordinary citizens was a painfully protracted and frustrating one, and so they waited patiently for the crisis to pass, hoping that the Nazis would soon lose their grip on power or that they would not enforce their threat to bar Jews from public life. They were not the only ones living on false hopes.

Persecution of Jews

For those who could not imagine leaving their homeland and turning their back on their friends and family for an unpredictable life in America, there was the vain hope that National Socialism was a temporary aberration, a storm that would eventually blow over. They imagined that Hitler's anti-Semitic laws did not apply to them, but only to the 40,000 impoverished *Ostjuden* who had fled the Russian pogroms and now lived in comparative squalor in the poor quarter of the city. The *Ostjuden* held fiercely to their customs, their Yiddish language and their 'exotic' orthodox clothing, which made them stand out as 'aliens' in the cosmopolitan capital and earned them the contempt of some of their non-observant brethren.

The Goldschlags were cultured and proud of the degree to which they could be said to have assimilated themselves into German society. Like many of their Jewish neighbours, they laughed at anti-Semitic jokes and in doing so felt themselves to be a special class; 'weekend Jews' who only observed the high holidays but otherwise lived no differently than the other residents in their apartment block. They were clearly embarrassed to be reminded that they shared a tradition with these 'outcasts'.

Besides, Stella's father, Gerhard, had fought for the Fatherland in the Great War. Surely, the regime would make a concession because of his service. It therefore came as a shock when he was dismissed from his position in 1935 in a purge of Jews from public posts ordered by Dr Goebbels and forced to make a precarious living as a composer. Most of his music was never performed and he sank into despair. Stella blamed the family's declining fortunes on the Jewish critics who derided her father's work as derivative and on the Jewish musical community who failed to recognize his talent. He was more philosophical, blaming his lack of success on changing tastes, which only made his proud and haughty daughter more resentful and determined to retaliate in some way. She was evidently ashamed of being Jewish and according to a close acquaintance was afraid of being 'publicly exposed' as a Jew, 'when she didn't look or feel Jewish'.

That same year Stella was informed she would no longer be allowed to attend the state school and would have to enrol at a private institution exclusively for Jews, established by a discharged teacher, Dr Leonore Goldschmidt, from whom she would have to seek a scholarship as her parents could not afford the fees. This embittered her further, prompting her to repeatedly deny that she was Jewish, although her classmates and the neighbourhood children knew otherwise. Now in her early teens, she nurtured a burning ambition to be a jazz singer and she had the voice and the looks to be another Dietrich, but again her 'Jewish blood' barred her from pursuing her dreams and she became indignant and 'difficult'.

She began to flaunt her sexuality and boasted of her many conquests, which none of her girlfriends could be sure were entirely fictitious. She was a convincing fantasist and was occasionally reproved by her teachers for frightening the younger girls with her lurid erotic tales and graphic sexual confessions. 'We were all Eves,' one of her former classmates admitted to author Peter Wyden, 'and she was the serpent.'

By the age of 16 she had a boyfriend, Manfred Kubler, the son of a wealthy businessman in whose home she and other young Jews would socialize, having been forbidden from attending clubs, cafes, cinemas and dance halls under the Nazi race laws. In October 1941 Manfred would become the first of her four husbands.

Gestapo recruit

She had managed to evade compulsory war work by studying fashion drawing and posing as a nude model at a local art school, but after her marriage she was ordered to report for work in a munitions factory and be registered as an 'armaments Jew'. She worked alongside her mother and in February 1943 the pair managed to avoid deportation because the Gestapo did not believe Jews could be blond. Her mother, Toni, had dyed her hair to match her daughter's, which was itself a crime.

That July she was arrested for having obtained false identity papers and was given the choice of leading them to the forger, Guenther Rogoff, or being transported along with her parents to Auschwitz. According to her biographer and childhood acquaintance Peter Wyden, she was mercilessly beaten.

> They kicked both of [her] shins to the breaking point and kept beating the same spot on [her] spine. [She] was bleeding from [her] mouth, ears, and nose and couldn't eat for days … Three times they took the safety off a pistol and put it against [her] temple. Totally shattered, [she] lay unconscious on the floor.

Her will was broken. The threat of torture and disfigurement was more than she could bear, but she did not know where Rogoff could be found so her only bargaining chip was to offer to work for the Gestapo. Incredibly, she made two successful escape attempts before she was interrogated for the third time and 'turned', so she was not a willing and eager recruit, at least not at first. But it is said that she soon came to enjoy her task and the power it gave her over those she had despised for so long.

Stella had few close friends, but she thought nothing of turning them in if it helped her meet her target. One of these unfortunate acquaintances was Lieselotte Streszak, whom Stella would lose track of during the war years, meeting her again quite by chance in 1944 while shopping in their old neighbourhood. A few days later the unsuspecting Lilo opened her apartment door to see Stella and a male companion, probably her second husband and fellow *Greifer* or 'catcher' Rolf Isaacsohn, who were by now notorious traitors. They had come to arrest her and both were armed.

It is believed that at one point she lured 62 Jews from their hiding places. The total number of her victims is thought to be in the hundreds. Curiously, she continued to work for the Gestapo as a 'catcher' long after they reneged on their promise and deported her parents to Auschwitz. It was rumoured that she had been prepared to go to her death with her parents but that they had persuaded her to do anything to save herself. Whatever the truth, she willingly cooperated with the Gestapo and was responsible for the deaths of countless Germans, whose only 'crime' was to have been alive and Jewish at the wrong time in the wrong place.

She was well paid for her treachery. Each victim was worth 200 marks. In addition, her name was removed from the deportation lists and she had official Gestapo ID papers, which gave her the authority and privileges she believed that she had been entitled to since the day she was born.

A traitor's fate

She haunted cafes, cinemas and even graveyards in the hope of making her quota of catches, earning herself a second soubriquet: 'The Blonde Ghost'. Cemeteries were a particularly bountiful source of prey. Jewish spouses would lose their immunity the day their German husbands and wives died, so Stella would scour the obituaries columns in the Berlin papers and turn up at the funeral to make the arrest.

In the last months of the war she learned that she was pregnant and told the man she believed to be the father, one of her many lovers, but he had no interest in supporting a child and abandoned Stella to her fate. For months, she scavenged for food and shelter in the woods around Brandenburg, terrified that the Russians would arrest her and execute her for collaborating with the enemy. She managed to remain undetected until October 1945, when her daughter was born, but a nurse at the hospital denounced her to the Soviets. At three separate trials, she was sentenced to ten years' hard labour, but served only one of the terms. On her release, she disappeared and was thought to have died.

Her activities and fate might have remained unknown had it not been for a former classmate whose insatiable curiosity drove him on a long and often painful search for the truth. Thirteen-year-old Peter Wyden had been infatuated with Stella when they were both pupils at the Goldschmidt School in Berlin in 1937, whose curriculum had been devised specifically to prepare Jewish émigrés for imminent flight. However, that same year his family managed to emigrate to the United States and so spared themselves the fate that befell those whose parents lacked the financial resources to pay the extortionate Nazi 'exit tax' and acquire the necessary visas. Emigration was prohibited for German Jews in September 1941, the same month that wearing the Star of David in public became law. Incredibly, 346,000 out of a total of more than half a million German Jews did manage to avoid deportation to the camps, but not all of them survived.

EMIGRATION WAS PROHIBITED FOR GERMAN JEWS IN SEPTEMBER 1941, THE SAME MONTH THAT THE WEARING OF THE STAR OF DAVID IN PUBLIC BECAME LAW

In the 1990s Peter finally traced her to the West German town where she was living an anonymous life and confronted her with the evidence of her treachery, for which she had spent ten years in a Soviet Gulag during the Cold War. Even faced with her childhood admirer, a Jew, she stubbornly refused to acknowledge her duplicity and made no effort to conceal her vitriolic anti-Semitism. Peter gives the impression that the object of his former childhood infatuation was, and perhaps always had been, emotionally unstable. Two years after their strained meeting, Stella committed suicide.

Ironically, her daughter, Yvonne, was forcibly taken from her at the end of the war and adopted by Jewish foster parents. When she grew up she became an Israeli nurse who dedicated her life to caring for others as an act of atonement for her mother's crimes. She recognizes the features she inherited from the woman she refuses to acknowledge by the term 'mother' and attributes the rest to her father, whose identity she doesn't know. She doubts that Stella knew him either, but thinks he was probably 'one her kind'. Such is the indelible taint she bears that she periodically feels the need to articulate it. 'I am Yvonne, who had better not have been born.'

Annette Wagner – Hitler's eyes Down Under

There was something decidedly odd about Annette Wagner, a dark beauty and fashion expert with her own regional radio show on ABC Radio in northern Australia, though no one at the station could put their finger on it. Her accent was certainly unusual. A cross between Swiss (the country of her birth), English (where she had spent her childhood) and French, the language in which she prefaced each of her weekly broadcasts to thousands of housewives and working women in Sydney.

There couldn't have been many French-speaking residents of Australia in 1938 and yet Mrs Wagner insisted on beginning each broadcast by reading cables purportedly from Paris. Even those listeners with a smattering of the language were unable to make head nor tail of them. Her own grasp of French was poor, which aroused further suspicion. There were whispers at the network that Annette's 'fashion tips' were coded messages to other 'sleeper' agents with whom she was known to associate – spies who had insinuated themselves into Australian society years in advance of the imminent conflict.

The Wagner house in an exclusive suburb of the city had been under constant observation by the Australian secret service ever since it became known there were senior Nazi officials living openly in the same neighbourhood.

Neutralized threat

The Australian Nazi Party was considered a serious threat to national security. It was known that they had established a sabotage squad and had identified key targets in the centre of Sydney. They were closely linked to the Berlin-based Auslands-Organization, which reached out to Germans living abroad and reminded them that it was their patriotic duty to join the Party. The organization also monitored the activities of German-born anti-Nazis and pressured them to cease their activities or face the consequences, which their agents in each country would enforce. It was a volatile and potentially ugly situation in which die-hard Nazis such as Annette Wagner and her Alsace-born husband Robert were to have played a vital role, if left unhindered.

Annette, however, posed a double threat, for she was also fluent in Japanese, having previously held a translator post at the League of Nations in Geneva and at the Japanese Embassy in London. As an occidental white female, she would have been a highly valued recruit. Apart from very rare instances, Japanese spies were almost exclusively consular officials and Asian employees of Japanese-owned companies.

Suspicions were raised when male visitors to the bungalow in Clifton Gardens came under cover of darkness, bringing instructions from Berlin and payment for services rendered.

They were subsequently identified by the ever-watchful Australian Intelligence Service as crew members from the German merchant ships anchored in Newcastle harbour. Annette also made regular trips to the Hydro

Majestic Hotel in the Blue Mountains, where she met known Nazi sympathizers.

But what alarmed the intelligence services most was her intense interest in watching military manoeuvres, none of which had any bearing on her job at the radio station. And then there were her 'flying lessons', during which she took dozens of aerial photographs as her unsuspecting pilot cruised low over 'sensitive' sites such as the BHP steelworks and Newcastle harbour.

Strictly speaking, she was under no obligation to justify her activities as Australia was not at war at this time, but the country was acutely aware that Japan's military regime had ambitions to extend its influence in South East Asia and that its spies and fifth columnists could be active on Australian soil long before war was declared. And so Mrs Wagner was put under 24-hour surveillance.

When war was declared by Prime Minister Robert Gordon Menzies on 3 September 1939, all those without Australian citizenship were prohibited from working in the media, including Annette Wagner, who protested that she posed no threat to national security as she was a citizen of neutral Switzerland. However, the administration was adamant. There would be no exceptions. With her movements restricted and her daily routine under intense scrutiny, she was no longer useful to her Nazi paymasters. She left for Vichy France in January 1940 with her husband and there she worked for German intelligence until her arrest in 1946. While awaiting interrogation by the Paris police she leapt to her death from a third-floor window.

CHAPTER SEVEN

SS Wives

Potential SS wives were not only required to undergo a rigorous process to assess their suitability as the bride of an elite SS soldier, but they also had to attend a six-week motherhood course. It might be supposed that aspiring spouses would be put off by these tedious formalities, but for many the material benefits of belonging to the SS community made it all worthwhile. The selection process did not ensure compatibility, though, because the divorce rate was high.

For some SS wives, their appointed role of supporting their spouses and nurturing future warriors was not enough. They used their position to gratify their sadistic tendencies and could sometimes be even more brutal than their husbands.

Himmler had a vision of the ideal SS soldier: he should be a modern Siegfried possessing all the virtues of the Teutonic knights; a specimen of Aryan perfection in flawless physical shape and as hard as tempered steel. Such a man would require a suitable mate to produce the perfect Aryan offspring. She should be virtuous, loyal, obedient and self-sacrificing. Such creatures only existed in myths and fairy tales, but that did not deter Himmler from trying to breed a race of supermen to fill the ranks of his fallen heroes.

In reality, the SS fell far short of their desired chivalric archetype. It became a ruthless component of the Nazi extermination machine whose participation in some of the worst atrocities of the war saw it branded as a criminal organization by the Nuremberg War Crimes tribunal. Many of its members' wives also proved to fall short of Himmler's ideal.

Applying to become an SS wife involved the acquisition of suitable references as well as the usual documentary evidence of an unsullied Aryan blood line traceable through several generations. The RuSHA (Race and Settlement Main Office) forms included a questionnaire testifying to the suitability of the bride, which was to be completed by two credible character witnesses. They were asked to affirm that her family was finally financially sound, or otherwise, and that they were committed to the National Socialist cause. Another part of the questionnaire required them to evaluate her personality, specifically whether she was 'fond of children or not', 'reliable or unreliable', 'thrifty or extravagant', 'companionable or domineering', 'home loving or fickle' and 'addicted to cleaning'. They were reminded that it was their duty to disclose any discreditable traits or reservations they might have in recommending the bride as a suitable candidate for marriage.

> **ANNELIESE F. WAS 'CONSCIENTIOUS AND RELIABLE, DRESSED MODESTLY AND HAD A SERIOUS MANNER AT ALL TIMES'. SHE WAS ALSO 'TIDY AND HOUSE-PROUD'**

In the case of Anneliese F., who was applying to marry Dachau block leader Franz Muller, a neighbour wrote that she was 'conscientious and reliable', that she 'dressed modestly' and 'has a serious manner at all times'. Her parents were 'thrifty' and were early supporters of the Party, having hosted meetings in their pub. Furthermore, she was 'tidy' and 'house-proud' and was 'never seen to have spent her money frivolously'.

Divorce was common

Once the candidate's application had been approved she would be required to attend a six-week course in 'motherhood' run by the German Women's Bureau. Even after all the preliminary hurdles had been overcome there was no guarantee that the marriage would be a happy or fruitful one, as the SS divorce records attest.

In 1934 Michael Lippert, commander of the Dachau guard, filed for divorce from his wife Marie. He knew how to manipulate the facts to his advantage. Among the many indignities he claimed to have suffered was the wanton destruction of his framed portraits of the Führer, Reichsmarschall Goering and Reichsführer SS Himmler. In the eyes of the court this became no mere domestic squabble, but a political gesture of defiance, possibly even a treasonable act. Marie was also accused of having made disparaging remarks concerning her husband to young guards, who were said to have been disturbed and demoralized by her outbursts. More shocking still was her admission that after she discovered she was pregnant she had deliberately drunk herself into a state which she hoped would be injurious to her unborn child. She wanted to give birth to 'an idiot child', as she thought that was what her husband deserved. The divorce was granted and Marie was ordered to pay all costs.

In 1944, Dachau block leader Josef Voggesberger petitioned for divorce from his wife of 11 years, Cazilie. She had become bored with the regimen of camp life and had neglected her housekeeping duties to drink and flirt with local men. She was also accused of having an affair with a man from a nearby town and, most unforgivably, had repeatedly made disparaging remarks about her husband to his superior officers. The divorce was granted, but the blame was attributed to Voggesberger, as he had broken the unspoken code of the SS by having an affair with another woman and neglecting his wife.

The presence of women in the male-dominated environment inevitably led to bad blood between brother officers, despite their oath of undying allegiance. While serving at Dachau SS Obersturmführer Albert Breh, who would later be convicted by an SS tribunal of fraud, fell foul of another SS officer, Herbert Vollmer, from the cadet school at Bad Tölz. As a result, Vollmer concocted a false report about Breh's intended bride, Ingeborg R., portraying her as a woman who failed to meet the ideals of an SS bride. He concocted a history of sexual misconduct, financial felonies and discreditable personal vices that ensured the marriage application would be rejected. It was, but primarily on the grounds that Ingeborg only stood five feet tall in her stockinged feet, so she was several inches too short.

Duties of an SS wife

Although 240,000 women joined the SS by marrying one of Himmler's elite they did not do so in a perfunctory manner or as a matter of routine. They knew what the function and duties of the SS entailed. The majority of SS wives may have been poorly educated, but they were not entirely ignorant of the primary aim of the organization, which was to subjugate and enslave the 'inferior races' in the occupied East.

They were aware too of their own subordinate role in the 'natural hierarchy of the sexes', as defined by the SS magazine *Das Schwarze Korps*, issue 13:

The man is assigned naturally the spiritual direction of the family; he founds it, he leads it, he fights for it, he defends it. By contrast, the woman gives the family the inner attitude, she gives it soul; in quiet, rarely noticed fulfilment of her duties she upholds what the man created and builds the quiet motive in the family relationship.

Her duty as a 'hero mother' in the 'racial battle' was to nurture the future warriors and galvanize their resolve to fight and sacrifice themselves for the Fatherland; in doing so, she would find her true worth and destiny. It was a nonsensical romantic fantasy more in keeping with one of Richard Wagner's operas than reality and it is unlikely that every SS wife took it very seriously, but it was worth feigning allegiance to such a cause to obtain the material benefits of belonging to the SS community. After all, had Himmler not promised every loyal wife that she would rule as queen over a feudal paradise in the East when the war was won? And who among them could imagine that they would not do so?

Vera Wohlauf

Vera Wohlauf was an example of a fanatical Nazi who used her official status as the wife of an SS officer to insinuate herself into an operation, in order to gratify her psychotic compulsions. An aberrant personality, she took advantage of the Nazi policy which encouraged wives of serving SS officers to accompany their husbands into the occupied territories to the East. She hoped to see the supposedly 'racially inferior' *Untermenschen* (subhumans) at first hand and witness her husband organize their 'resettlement', a euphemism for extermination. He may have invited her along one day in order to impress her, but she evidently needed little encouragement to abuse that 'privilege' and became an active participant in the atrocities. However, her presence proved to have an unsettling effect on the men.

Several members of Captain Julius Wohlauf's Police Battalion 101 voiced their disapproval at seeing his pregnant bride climb into the front seat of a truck one morning on 25 August 1942, attired in a military coat and peaked cap. They were to take part in an *Aktion* – rounding up Polish Jews from the Międzyrzec-Podlaski ghetto for transportation to Treblinka. While some merely resented having their superior's wife tag along for the ride, as if it were a picnic, others were later to admit to feelings of embarrassment and even shame knowing that a woman was to witness their brutality. They needn't have worried. Frau Wohlauf was not easily shocked. In fact, she was visibly aroused by the obvious distress of their intended victims, whom she saw as rats running before the hounds.

Despite being four months pregnant at the time, she expressed no sympathy for the children who clung to their mothers and wept openly in fear of what awaited them. Those who were too slow, too frail or who resisted were beaten or shot dead on the spot. Others died of heat exhaustion as they waited in the main square for hour after hour in the broiling sun, with no food or water. Over the course of two days 960 bodies were left to rot after the remaining 11,000 inhabitants of the ghetto were locked into the cramped and airless cattle wagons bound for the death camp.

Although there were other women present – the wives of Nazi officials and Red Cross nurses – Vera Wohlauf was the only one to make her presence felt by walking through the huddled mass of people brandishing a horsewhip and taking every opportunity to heap further torment upon the cowering souls.

Curiously, it was Vera Wohlauf who appeared to be the enthusiastic Jew-baiter in these *Aktions*. Her husband, who was known as 'little Rommel' to the men because of his puffed-up self-importance, was not a rabid anti-Semite. While the wives and mistresses of Nazi officials chose to observe the distressing scene from a distance, Frau Wohlauf exhibited scant concern for her personal safety as she strode among the groups of Jews while stray bullets from drunken *Trawnikis* – the Ukrainian, Lithuanian and Latvian auxiliaries – whizzed in all directions.

Disturbed by a woman's presence

After the massacre, the battalion's commander, Major Trapp, made his feelings known regarding the presence of officer's wives at such operations and was particularly appalled to learn that Captain Wohlauf's wife was pregnant. Women in such a state should not have witnessed such scenes, he said, apparently ignorant of the fact that she had been anything but an innocent bystander.

Major Trapp was shocked that a symbol of German womanhood, the embodiment of the Nazi credo *Kirche, Küche und Kinder* (Church, Kitchen and Children), should be sullied by such unsavoury sights. And yet in spite of his explicit disapproval of her appearance at the Międzyrzec–Podlaski ghetto massacre, Frau Wohlauf remained with her husband's unit and took part in several more bloody '*Aktions*' in the following weeks.

Wendy Lower, author of *Hitler's Furies*, speculates that what perhaps disturbed Major Trapp and his men more than anything else was that Vera Wohlauf behaved like a man. And it was this 'intrusion' that some of the men under her husband's command objected to. It was simply against their perverse principles that a woman should have been permitted to participate in the brutal 'hunt' for Jews. They resented her incursion into their world and her presence reminded them of their own families and how they might react to seeing their sons and fathers behaving in a bestial manner.

Great pains had been taken by the SS to create a semblance of normality for the men, so that they could carry out their murderous task day in and day out and never question their actions or their orders. A programme of cultural and social activities was provided, sports events were organized and religious services were held, which had the effect of sanctioning the killings. It was therefore acceptable for women to witness these activities, but not to take part in the operations.

Those who said no

It has been assumed that every member of these killing units behaved in the same way and therefore Vera Wohlauf's behaviour might have been attributed to 'battlefield frenzy' – a temporary collective insanity – but even in such a heightened state of anti-Semitic hysteria not everyone in these police battalions acted on impulse. An internal investigation by a police officer into a massacre at the Marcinkance ghetto in the Bialystok district revealed that only four or five of the 17-man unit were what are known as 'eager killers'. Another six or seven men stood by the perimeter, as they had been ordered to do, to shoot anyone who attempted to escape. Three men didn't fire their weapons during the entire operation, while a fourth refused to participate. A fifth committed suicide the night before, knowing that he would be ordered to kill civilians. None refused on moral grounds. Their complaint was mainly that the sight of so much wanton slaughter made them physically sick and therefore unable to function. The investigation had been instigated because it was claimed that there had been armed resistance to the round-up, which prompted the unit to fire into the panicking throng, killing 132 of them.

In another incident, the commander of Police Battalion 306, Klaus Horning, refused to obey an order to execute 800 Soviet POWs on the grounds that members of police units were obligated under military law to refuse to carry out criminal orders. He was sentenced to six months in prison by a German military court, giving the lie to the claim made by countless war criminals that they would have been shot if they had refused to obey orders. David H. Kitterman, author of *Those Who Said No!*, cited 100 documented cases in which members of the Wehrmacht, the police and even the Einsatzgruppen refused to obey an order to execute POWs. They received nominal sentences, reprimands and other token penalties, such as being reassigned to less arduous duties.

> **TWO-THIRDS OF THE MEN WHO REFUSED TO OBEY AN ORDER TO EXECUTE POWS WERE SHOCKED TO LEARN THERE WERE NO CONSEQUENCES TO THEIR REFUSAL**

Two-thirds of the men were shocked to learn that there were no consequences to their refusal, even though they had expected to be shot for doing so.

Otto Bradfisch, the head of Einsatzkommando 8, informed his men that anyone who could not perform their duties because it did not sit right with their conscience was not obliged to take part in the executions of their Soviet prisoners. As Kitterman observed:

> In every case of documented refusal to obey orders to exterminate people, the coercive powers of the Nazi system proved to be impotent or ineffective.

CHAPTER EIGHT

Women Behind the Wire

Many thousands of women were incarcerated by the Nazis in various institutions during the Second World War. Around 130,000 women and children passed through Ravensbrück alone between 1939 and 1945, the majority of them political prisoners. Jews were in the minority.

Those who were not murdered were kept in the harshest and most appalling conditions. But these were not the only hazards. A number of women were unnecessarily operated on without anaesthetic by evil doctors, under the pretext of conducting valid research. Those who did not die were maimed or crippled for life.

But not all women suffered in these camps. Some of the wives of the SS overseers took the opportunity to help themselves to the valuables that had been brought in by the prisoners.

The camps also provided the women who had been appointed as camp guards with an outlet for their latent sadistic tendencies. Most of them were from the lower classes, without education or prospects, and some of these made the most of their new-found power by making life an even greater hell for the unfortunate women who were now at their mercy.

Thousands of German women, many of them Aryans as defined by Nazi law, spent the Hitler years behind barbed wire, their sole crime being their passive, non-violent opposition to the regime. They were not Jews, nor were they designated as being 'undesirables' (i.e. Romany Gypsies, lesbians, alcoholics and the 'racially inferior', such as Poles and Slavs), but they were merely ideologically opposed to National Socialism. Some were political opponents, Communists or Social Democrats, others were members of religious groups such as Jehovah's Witnesses, who were judged to be 'enemies of the state'. The latter were persecuted because their beliefs prohibited them from swearing an oath of allegiance to the administration, giving the obligatory 'Heil Hitler' salute and joining the German armed forces. They were among the first to be rounded up and incarcerated in the early forced labour camps.

Sadly, the bitter enmity between the Social Democrats and the Communists, which had enabled the Nazis to seize power, continued in the camps and discouraged cooperation between the two factions. There were even instances where mutual distrust led members of one group to denounce those in the rival group. This animosity was frequently exploited by their guards, who stirred up resentment by deliberately appointing members of one group to be Kapos, or trustees, in preference to the other.

Moringen and Lichtenburg

Centa Beimler was a leading Communist in Moringen, Lower Saxony and the wife of a resistance hero who had escaped from Dachau. In 1933, she was interned in Stadelheim Prison near Munich, where the Nazis guillotined their political enemies, and she spent almost three years pacing her tiny cell trying to shake off the thought that she might be next. Her torment was aggravated by anxiety for her husband, Hans, who had volunteered to fight Franco's fascists in Spain as part of the International Brigade.

In early 1936, she was transferred to the Moringen workhouse for women, where the prisoners were permitted to wear their own clothes and were not subjected to the beatings meted out to their male comrades in the forced labour camps. In contrast, the 90 female inmates of Moringen were occupied for eight hours a day repairing clothes, but they were able to talk among themselves and move freely in the communal rooms and dormitories. Moringen operated as a Prussian state prison under the authority of a civilian director, whose sole function was to instil order.

When Hans was killed in the winter of 1936, Centa was considered to be of no further use to the Nazis as a hostage and was released. Her fellow detainees were transferred the following winter to Lichtenburg, an imposing Renaissance castle near Wittenberg which had become vacant after its male population had been transported elsewhere. Himmler made an inspection of the Moringen workhouse in May 1937 and came to the conclusion that the regime was too lenient and that the female prison population was only going to grow in the coming years. Rehabilitation was not the purpose of the exercise. These women were to be removed permanently from the population and a secure prison was required to house them. Lichtenburg was deemed to be suitable and by the spring of 1939 over 1,000 female inmates were incarcerated behind its formidable walls and subjected to a stricter regime administered by the SS.

Thirty-year-old Jehovah's Witness Erna Ludolph was among the initial intake and was soon under the impression that the 400 or so Witnesses were singled out for harsher treatment because of their beliefs. Forced labour became a greater part of the monotonous daily routine and punishments for even the most basic infractions were more severe. When Erna and the other Jehovah's Witnesses refused to assemble to hear a Party propaganda broadcast they were physically assaulted and soaked with high-pressure hoses.

Lichtenburg was closed down for unstated reasons in May 1939 and its inmates were transported to Ravensbrück, 50 miles north of Berlin.

Ravensbrück

'Ravensbrück was an abomination that the world has resolved to forget.'

François Mauriac, French Nobel Prize-winning novelist

Ravensbrück was a concentration camp exclusively for women, where the male SS guards and the female overseers presided over a brutal, punitive regime in which the prisoners were routinely worked to death and beaten or died from dehydration, starvation and disease.

Only a minority of those detained without trial or appeal were Jews (less than 20 per cent). The majority were political prisoners or petty criminals, although the Nazi definition of what constituted a criminal offence was highly questionable. Some had been interned merely because they had undergone abortions or had been forced into prostitution (both of which had been criminalized under the regime). A proportion had been convicted of violating the Nazi race laws, which prohibited sexual relations between Jews and Aryans. However, all were categorized as 'deviants' or 'social outcasts' and issued with identical blue and grey striped dresses and a headscarf and subjected to rigid discipline, which was designed to degrade and dehumanize them.

Conditions were spartan in the extreme, sanitation facilities and hygiene were crude and the overcrowded, unheated living conditions were unfit for animals. The women were packed into barracks like battery hens, where disease was allowed to run unchecked and was even seen as a convenient means of thinning out those unfit for work. Thirst, hypothermia and malnutrition reduced their number further. Others were murdered; executed by hanging, lethal injection, gas (in the portable gas chamber) or shot to death in the narrow alley known as the 'shooting gallery'. At least 86 healthy young women were subjected to sadistic experiments, as a result of which they either died or were maimed for life.

The eminent French anthropologist Germaine Tillion, who managed to smuggle out the names of key SS personnel encoded as recipes, described the camp, 50 miles north of Berlin, as 'a world of horror ... more terrifying than the visions of Dante'.

WOMEN HAD TO STAND SILENT FOR UP TO FOUR HOURS IN THEIR BARE FEET AND DISOBEDIENCE WAS PUNISHED BY FLOGGING OR SUMMARY EXECUTION

The twice daily roll calls, for which the women had to stand still and silent for up to four hours at a time in their bare feet, were introduced to instil regimentation and disobedience was punished by flogging or summary execution. The arduous work, inhuman treatment and 'neurotically enforced cleaning routines' (a description attributed to German Communist Margarete Buber Neumann) were intended to reduce the prisoner's sense of self-worth to zero and break her spirit.

Margarete had endured the privations of the Russian Gulags before she was transported along with 350 other former Soviet prisoners to Ravensbrück in 1940, a victim of Stalin's 'goodwill gesture' under the Nazi–Soviet pact. She was then one of just over 3,000 female prisoners housed in two dozen barracks surrounded by an electrified fence.

Around 1.6 million people were being kept in the Gulags immediately before the Second World War. As well as robbers, rapists and murderers the Gulags held political prisoners and many who had committed very minor 'crimes' such as making jokes about the regime or being late for work or absent without reason. Still more were innocents who had been caught up in the frequent purges of the secret police. One of the main purposes of the Gulags was to provide forced labour to man the camp factories and build roads and railways. Death rates were high, many dying from the extreme cold, violence, malnutrition, disease and hard labour.

In her memoir, *Under Two Dictators*, Margarete describes her initial relief at finding the conditions and facilities at Ravensbrück a degree or two less primitive than the Gulag, but she soon revises her opinion.

> Christian morality declares that suffering ennobles the sufferer. That can be only a very qualified truth. Life in a concentration camp showed the contrary to be true more often than not. I think that nothing is more demoralizing than suffering, excessive suffering coupled with humiliation such as comes to men and women in concentration camps ... You had lost all human rights – all, all without exception. You were just a living being with a number to distinguish you from the other unfortunates around you.

Despite having shared their suffering, she was shunned by her fellow Communists, who regarded her as a Trotskyist and refused to hear any criticism of the Soviet state or of her harrowing experiences in the Gulags. Instead, she was adopted by the female Jehovah's Witnesses, who believed Hitler was the Antichrist. Their faith helped sustain her in the darkest hours, when the crematorium was operating day and night. But she was more fortunate than some. As a German and a non-Jew she was excused from the more arduous work details and was instead assigned the duties of block supervisor, which meant she was watching over her fellow inmates, for which she received increased rations and other privileges.

Inmates were routinely terrorized by vicious guard dogs in the belief that women were more intimidated by them than men and could be herded like frightened sheep to work or slaughter.

Untold atrocities

Ravensbrück was used as a model for the women's camp at Auschwitz and was initially constructed to hold 5,000 inmates, but it was soon expanded to 40 sub-camps containing 45,000 prisoners and with the overcrowding came a marked deterioration in living conditions and an increase in executions and random killings. In April 1941, a separate camp for teenage girls who had been categorized as 'delinquents' was opened at Uckermark. In addition, there were an estimated 800 children living behind the barbed wire, some of whom had been born in the camp. After Auschwitz was abandoned, the remaining Jewish women prisoners were taken to Ravensbrück to be murdered in the portable gas chamber that had recently been installed on the site.

Just days after Margarete's release on 21 April 1945, thanks to the intervention of the Red Cross, some 20,000 remaining prisoners were herded on a forced march, which saw more of them dying by the roadside from starvation and exhaustion. An additional 2,000 sick and malnourished prisoners were left to die in the deserted compound. During its six-year operation an estimated 132,000 women from eastern Europe as well as from France, Belgium, Britain and Scandinavia were imprisoned at Ravensbrück, of whom only 15,000 are believed to have survived. Just under 20 per cent were German or Austrian citizens. Among these were artists, academics, doctors, writers, politicians and intellectuals.

The scale of the atrocities and the final number of victims will never be known, because the Germans destroyed the official records shortly before the camp's liberation, while historians were denied access to whatever documents

Among those sent to Ravensbrück was Geneviève de Gaulle, niece of Charles de Gaulle, whom Himmler ordered to be kept in isolation in the hope that she might be a bargaining chip when it came to saving his skin at the end of the war. Incredibly, Himmler even ordered the imprisonment of his own sister, Olga, as punishment for having an affair with a Polish officer, but she was released shortly afterwards. She had presumably promised not to incur her brother's displeasure in the future.

It was, incidentally, on Himmler's orders that the camp zoo and aviary were constructed and flower beds created at the entrance; he hoped that the Red Cross and visiting dignitaries would get the impression that it was a model camp. Inmates were paid a nominal wage for their work so that the Nazis could claim that they were not slaves, although that is effectively what they were.

The Reichsführer SS inspected the camp himself on several occasions, combining a sightseeing tour with a visit to his mistress, who lived nearby.

had survived until after the fall of the Berlin Wall. The East German authorities ignored the presence of Catholic women, Jews and Jehovah's Witnesses and instead played up the role of the camp's working-class women to create a highly selective history of Ravensbrück, which served the Soviet state's political agenda.

The evil of Dr Oberheuser

Dr Herta Oberheuser could not claim to lack intelligence, education or privilege and yet she betrayed the principles of her profession in the relentless pursuit of personal advancement.

Dr Oberheuser was a dermatologist, but she wanted to be a surgeon. Ravensbrück gave her the opportunity and the authority to conduct medical experiments for which she was neither competent nor qualified. Her vile and unnecessary operations were carried out on 72 terrified Polish Catholics without anaesthetic under the pretext of testing the efficacy of sulphanilamide on battle wounds. Healthy unwilling prisoners had limbs amputated and parts of bone, muscle and tissue were removed so that Dr Oberheuser could study nerve and tissue regeneration. Sulphanilamide was first prepared in 1908 by Austrian chemist Paul Gelmo. It proved to be a very effective antibacterial agent and was applied to wounds by the Allies as well as the Germans in the Second World War, dramatically reducing mortality rates.

> UNDER THE PRETEXT OF TESTING SULPHANILAMIDE ON BATTLE WOUNDS, PRISONERS HAD LIMBS AMPUTATED AND BONE, MUSCLE AND TISSUE REMOVED

The sadistic 'tests' had been initiated after the assassination of Himmler's deputy, SS-Obergruppenführer Reinhard Heydrich, in 1942. The ruthless Heydrich, who had earned the nickname 'Hitler's Hangman' for his pitiless treatment of the Czechs, died from blood poisoning after fibres from the upholstery of the car he was travelling in at the time of the attack entered his open wounds.

Himmler's personal physician, Dr Karl Gebhardt, had refused to administer sulpha drugs which might have saved his patient and as a result Himmler sanctioned experiments on Ravensbrück prisoners in order to prove to Hitler that Gebhardt had been right to do so. It was Gebhardt who devised the experiments which were carried out by his assistant Dr Oberheuser, who inflicted identical wounds on her human guinea pigs and inserted shards of glass, fibres, dirt, rusty nails, sawdust and bacteria into the wounds before sewing them up and awaiting the result.

Sadistic experiments

Dr Oberheuser had previously worked at Auschwitz, where she had been accused of injecting healthy children with oil and Evipan, before amputating their limbs and removing their vital organs. Evipan, introduced by Bayer AG in 1933, was a widely-used anaesthetic, but its misuse by the evil Dr Oberheuser caused the rapid death of the children.

The women of Ravensbrück had been chosen for experimentation in the belief that they would be easier to subdue than men. They were treated in groups of ten at a time and when their allotted time had elapsed and the results had been recorded the survivors would be executed. Those who could no longer walk were carried. At the 'shooting gallery' they would do what they could to make themselves presentable, doing each other's hair and pinching their cheeks to bring a touch of colour to their pallid skin in order to die with dignity and self-respect.

For those who still had the strength, their last act of defiance would be to refuse the sedative offered by their guards so they could cry out 'Long Live Poland' before they were killed.

In the final months of the war, a rumour circulated around the camp that the survivors were to be executed to eradicate all traces of the experiments, but on the night they were due to be shot some Russian prisoners cut the power and the women were able to scatter to concealed hiding places throughout the camp.

After the liberation of Ravensbrück there wasn't much the Red Cross could do for the survivors of the sulpha 'tests', but in 1958 a Connecticut philanthropist, Caroline Ferriday, raised public awareness and sufficient funds to take 35 of the women to America for treatment.

Stanislawa 'Stasha' Sledziejowska-Osiczko, now in her seventies, was one of the fortunate ones to be given that lifeline. Despite all that she suffered she sees no point in hating her oppressors. 'I don't hold a grudge,' she said. 'I forgive them completely.'

Testimony of a victim

On 20 December 1946, Vladislava Karolewska, a 35-year-old former schoolteacher from Grudenz, testified at Nuremberg about the treatment she received under Oberheuser.

Vladislava and the other Polish patients were confined in a locked ward and were not told the nature or purpose of their operation. After being wheeled into the operating room she lost consciousness and awoke the next morning with a high temperature and in considerable pain, but she was given nothing to alleviate it. Her lower leg was in a cast and the whole leg was swollen from the toes to the groin. The pain increased during the day and on the next day pus was seeping from a wound. It was then that she underwent a second very painful procedure under Dr Fischer, who cut something out of her leg while Dr Oberheuser observed.

> Two weeks later we were all taken again to the operating room and put on the operating tables. The bandage was removed, and that was the first time I saw my leg. The incision went so deep that I could see the bone ... On the eighth of September I was sent back to the block. I could not walk. The pus was draining from my leg; the leg was swollen up and I could not walk. In the block, I stayed in bed for one week; then I was called to the hospital again.

Unable to walk, she had to be carried by her comrades. Outside they could see an ambulance which the Germans used to transport patients who were to be executed, so they feared that they were to be shot; but instead they were told by Dr Oberheuser to get dressed and walk unaided to the operating room, where their dressings would be changed. In spite of being in considerable pain, Vladislava and the other women stumbled to the operating room only to be told by Dr Oberheuser that the change of dressings would not take place after all.

When they were later told that they were to be operated on yet again, Vladislava replied that she would rather be shot.

Unimaginable torture
At the end of February 1943, they were forcibly subjected to yet another operation.

> Dr Trommel took me by the left wrist and pulled my arm back. With his other hand he tried to gag me, putting a piece of rag into my mouth, because I shouted. The second SS man took my right hand and stretched it. Two other SS men held me by my feet. Immobilized, I felt that somebody was giving me an injection. I defended myself for a long time, but then I grew weaker. The injection had its effect; I felt sleepy.

I heard Trommel saying, '*Das ist fertig*', that is all. I regained consciousness again, but I don't know when. Then I noticed that a German nurse was taking off my dress. I then lost consciousness again; I regained it in the morning. Then I noticed that both my legs were in iron splints and were bandaged from the toes to the groin. I felt a strong pain in my feet, and a temperature ... Two weeks later a second operation was performed on my left leg although pus was draining from my former wound, and a piece of shin bone was removed.

Under cross-examination, Dr Oberheuser attempted to defend her actions by claiming that she had been told by Professor Gebhardt, that the operations

had been ordered on the highest level, that the state had ordered it, and that it was legal and, in any case, that the experiments were not supposed to be dangerous, and besides, that they were Poles who had been sentenced to death.

She denied too that the procedures conducted without anaesthetic caused her victims pain.

I do not believe that the patients suffered that much; because they never expressed any kind of disagreement, either with the treatment by Professor Gebhardt, or by Dr Fischer. I myself never had any difficulties, but always believed that they were pleased with my care ... only a few of them were seriously injured because the others healed very quickly and the disease pattern was actually just that of a boil.

She also denied administering lethal injections of petroleum ether to kill 'patients' who had outlived their usefulness.

Dr Oberheuser was the only female physician to be indicted at the Nuremberg Doctors' Trial, which began on 9 December 1946, during which she and her co-defendants were charged with 'murders, brutalities cruelties, tortures, atrocities and other inhuman acts'. The trial ended on 20 August 1947, after testimony had been heard from 85 witnesses and the content of 1,471 contemporary documents had been taken into account. She was subsequently found guilty and sentenced to 20 years' imprisonment, but she only served five years before being released in April 1952. She then became a family doctor in West Germany until she was identified by a former inmate in 1956 and lost her position. Her licence was revoked in 1958.

Profiting from distress

On 28 April 1945 a Swiss Red Cross worker witnessed the evacuation of Ravensbrück concentration camp ahead of the advancing Russians. Ragged columns of several thousand male and female inmates were being herded in a westerly direction by SS men and female guards. At the head of one column a small wagon was being hauled by six emaciated female prisoners, their bones clearly visible through their skin. Sitting on the wagon among her belongings sat a smartly dressed overweight woman, the wife of an SS guard, who had earlier complained of stomach cramps. The Red Cross worker learned that her digestive problems were due to her having gorged herself on food from Red Cross parcels that had been intended for the prisoners.

> **THE SS GUARD'S WIFE'S DIGESTIVE PROBLEMS WERE DUE TO HER HAVING GORGED HERSELF ON FOOD INTENDED FOR THE PRISONERS**

Such women managed to vanish into the general population in the chaotic aftermath of the war and resume their small, anonymous lives without fear of recrimination.

They were not war criminals but *Mitlaufer*, or 'fellow travellers', as defined under the Allied denazification process: that is, Nazi supporters who had not directly taken part in any atrocities. However, they were in their own small, insignificant way an essential element of the Nazis' terror apparatus. They profited by it and saw nothing wrong in doing so. For example, Hildegard Bischoff, the wife of SS Sturmbannführer Karl Bischoff, acquired a considerable amount of looted valuables during the two and half years her husband served as the chief of construction at Auschwitz.

Maria Pawela, a young Polish worker assigned to work in the household, recalled watching Frau Bischoff packing in April 1944 before the couple left for Katowice, where Karl had been appointed chief of the building bureau for the Waffen SS.

> The Bischoffs had a lot of gold and valuables. I only saw this before they left Oswiecim. When she was packing their things, she took out two quite large tin chests … full of gold and a few clothes …

Other wives regularly found themselves the recipients of gifts of silver cutlery, porcelain, china, jewellery, watches and fur coats; all 'abandoned' by the new arrivals during the selection process and there for the taking.

Wielding power

Prakseda Witek, a 14-year-old Polish worker, recalled another SS couple who were not choosy about what they appropriated:

> The Kitts … brought lots of things home from the camp. Every so often they sent off to Germany a large steamer trunk full of the most various valuables, material, perfumes, soaps and so forth.

In a totalitarian regime such nonentities suddenly found themselves wielding power over their neighbours, as well as people who would have been higher up the social scale only a few years earlier.

Not all SS wives were as lacking in compassion. Inmate Aleksandra Stawarczyk, who worked in the household of Dr Horst Fischer, remembered seeing Frau Fischer offering the prisoners cigarettes, 'and when they were working in the garden in the rain or cold she instructed me to give them something warm to drink, and some bread'.

It has been the norm to condemn only the men who played an active role in Nazi crimes and marginalize civilian women as either 'fellow travellers' or passive bystanders. The myth of their inculpability was adopted by a post-war culture which could not conceive of good, God-fearing German women as anything other than dutiful mothers and devoted daughters, a romanticized image perpetuated by SS veterans' organizations and even the Catholic women's periodical *Der Regenbogen*.

Even lowly civil servants played a vital and deleterious role in implementing Hitler's racist policies. Walter H. Schneider remembers his female teacher, Fräulein Krappot, publicly ridiculing his part-Jewish friend during the war years, until the boy and his mother committed suicide.

SS auxiliaries

SS men occupied all the senior posts at Ravensbrück, with the women employed as guards and subordinate to them. Himmler would not countenance admitting women to the SS, but once the war was under way he finally agreed to compromise by granting them admission as SS auxiliaries (*Gefolge*). Most of the female camp personnel were volunteers and professed to have no particular political affiliation or interest and many were not even Party members. They were almost all single women who had been attracted by the prospect of a secure job with reasonable pay, free accommodation, regular meals and the possibility of advancement in the ranks. Few had any professional or academic qualifications and almost all of them came from the lower social classes, with no prospect of better wages or job security in the outside world. It could be argued that their lack of education and disadvantaged backgrounds made them more malleable and even in some extreme cases vindictive, so they were more prone to take out their frustration on those powerless women in their charge.

CHAPTER NINE

A Monster is Brought to Justice

'Absolute power corrupts absolutely', according to the nineteenth-century politician Lord Acton, and nowhere was this truer than in the concentration camps, where female guards were allowed free licence over the prisoners. Some of these women took sadism to new levels, but the cruelty of one of their number almost surpasses belief. Killing children before their mothers' eyes, murdering victims by stamping on their faces and whipping women to death are only some of her many crimes.

What turned a girl with a strict religious education into an evil monster? Could it happen to anyone with a predisposition to cruelty who is given absolute power over their fellow human beings? Or did the regime attract an uncommonly large number of sadists and psychopaths?

In an amazing twist of fate, after the war

one of the perpetrators was discovered living the life of a normal housewife in a New York borough, and brought to justice.

Hermine Braunsteiner spent her days sewing dolls and soft toys, although she had no children to give them to. None came to see her either, although she was now in her sixties and might have been expected to have had grandchildren of her own. But it passed the time. And she had time to kill.

Hermine Ryan, the first American citizen to be extradited for war crimes, had been sentenced to life imprisonment in West Germany in 1981 for murder. Two of her female victims had been named on the indictment, but she had brutalized and killed countless women and children while serving as assistant warden at the notorious Majdanek death camp, on the outskirts of Lublin in eastern Poland, between October 1942 and spring 1944.

At her trial in Dusseldorf, which began on 26 November 1975 and ended on 30 June 1981, witnesses described seeing her whipping women to death, kicking away a stool to hang a 14-year-old Polish girl and seizing children by the hair and throwing them on to the trucks that conveyed them to the gas chamber. But her preferred method of execution was kicking her helpless victims to death by stamping on their faces with her steel-capped jack boots. It earned her the nickname the 'Stomping Mare'.

She might have remained an anonymous housewife in a blue-collar neighbourhood in Queens had Joseph Lelyveld, a cub reporter from

> **WITNESSES SAW BRAUNSTEINER WHIPPING WOMEN TO DEATH, KICKING AWAY A STOOL TO HANG A 14-YEAR-OLD AND SENDING KIDS TO THE GAS CHAMBER**

the *New York Times*, not followed up a lead from the Viennese Nazi-hunter Simon Wiesenthal back in the summer of 1964.

Simon Wiesenthal had vowed to track down those responsible for the genocide of the Jews. He had survived incarceration in four camps and his wife Cyla was a survivor of Janowska camp in Poland. When three former female inmates of Majdanek approached him in January 1964 with details of Braunsteiner's crimes and pleaded with him to bring her to justice, Wiesenthal sent an associate to locate her.

It was an easier task than Lelyveld had expected. The first Mrs Ryan who answered her door was immediately able to point him in the direction of the second, when asked if she knew of a recent arrival with the same surname and a heavy German accent.

After knocking at the door of 54–44 82nd Street, Lelyveld was confronted with an unnerving sight. The person who answered the door was not the grim-faced concentration camp guard he had expected, but a typical suburban housewife in pink and white striped shorts and matching sleeveless blouse, her hair in curlers and a paintbrush in her hand.

'There was nothing frightening about her,' he remembered, when interviewed decades later for *California Conversations*, an online magazine. 'That, I guess, is the whole horror of the Holocaust; perfectly ordinary people turning into psychopathic killers.'

Carried a horsewhip

'Mrs Ryan, I need to ask you about your time in Poland, at the Majdanek camp, during the war.' These were the words the tall, large-boned stern-faced Austrian had feared she would hear one day, but it was still a shock.

'Oh, my God, I knew this would happen,' she said, breaking into sobs. 'You've come.'

She was still struggling to recover her composure as she began reciting the 'weepy, self-pitying' defence she had been rehearsing in her mind the past few years, while they sat in her neat and orderly living room with its Alpine pictures and cuckoo clock, that stifling July afternoon.

Lelyveld, son of a prominent Rabbi and a future editor of the *New York Times*, had only the vaguest idea of the nature and extent of her crimes at that time, but he was already familiar with the evasion, excuses and bare-faced lies former Nazis had prepared to fend off accusations of their part in war-time atrocities. The Eichmann trial had concluded only two years earlier and the image of the impassive, bespectacled Nazi functionary was not something Jews of his generation would forget.

'Mrs Ryan' readily admitted to being Hermine Braunsteiner, but claimed that she had only been a guard at the camp and had 'no authority'. 'All I did is what guards do in camps now,' she tried to assure him. She resented being 'bothered' and protested that she believed she had been 'punished enough' for her alleged crimes, for which she had served three years in an Austrian prison. She maintained that she had been at Majdanek for only a year and had spent eight months in the infirmary as a patient, a story which was subsequently exposed as a lie. In fact, she had been the assistant commandant and one of 'the most vicious' according to a survivor. Often seen carrying a horsewhip, with which she frequently lashed female prisoners, she was said to have taken 'particular joy' in finding extra victims for the gas chambers and would tear children and infants from their mother's arms to fulfil the daily quota.

She took an active and uncommon interest in the selection process at the camps when new arrivals were weeded out – one group was consigned to slave labour and the rest were sent to die in the gas chambers. During one selection session, Braunsteiner heard crying coming from a man's backpack after she had struck at him with her whip. He had been protecting a child, who was immediately killed.

'Wouldn't hurt a fly'

It was Wiesenthal's belief that outwardly 'ordinary' men and women like Braunsteiner would discover their 'latent sadistic inclinations' when given power over others in such camps. But when divested of their authority and faced with their unspeakable cruelty they would affect a meek demeanour and protest that they were incapable of such things. 'Mrs Ryan' was certainly performing to type.

She had evidently fooled her American husband, electrician Russell Ryan, who had believed her when she told him she had been conscripted into the prison service and that she 'had not been in charge of anything'. He called Lelyveld later that same day to counter the accusations with the pitiful defence: 'Let the dead rest.' But how could they when their tormentor and her ilk were free and living lives that they had denied to their victims?

> BRAUNSTEINER HAD HER HUSBAND FOOLED. 'MY WIFE WOULDN'T HURT A FLY,' RYAN ASSERTED. 'THERE IS NO MORE DECENT PERSON ON THIS EARTH.'

'My wife wouldn't hurt a fly,' Ryan asserted. 'There is no more decent person on this earth.'

When she was formally identified and her past became public knowledge, her neighbours all expressed astonishment that such an apparently affable old woman could have been responsible for so much needless suffering. More than one remarked on her fastidious housework, as if it mitigated her documented acts of sadism.

In 1964 the 'Holocaust' was a term just coming into common usage to describe the genocide of the Jews and there were only a few reliable sources a reporter could consult. However, *The Black Book: The Nazi Crime Against the Jewish People* was to be found in the New York Times editorial library. Lelyveld later wrote that:

> Those accounts gave the lie to her own self-portrait of a hapless young conscript convalescing in the infirmary. She was one of a small number of female SS guards at Majdanek who had been charged with acts of extreme cruelty, even by the ferocious standards of the place ... she headed the list of wardresses responsible for 'unparalleled atrocities'.

Hermine Braunsteiner (or Braunstein as she was known then) 'figured prominently' in the testimony of Majdanek survivors. 'I myself saw babies taken from their mothers and killed before their eyes,' a witness was quoted as saying.
Lelyveld went on to say that:

> According to some of the materials I found during my later research, she seems to have done some monstrous things ... Of course, there is no justice in these matters. There can never be any justice ... There is no such thing as restitution in regards to the Holocaust.

An estimated 360,000 people had been murdered at Majdanek. The majority were Polish Jews, but there were also German, French and Dutch citizens transported from the occupied countries. When the wind was strong, the stench of sickness, decay and burning flesh drifted towards the city. The inhabitants of Lublin would have been unable to deny what had taken place within sight of their homes.

Career path of a monster
Hermine Braunsteiner was born in Austria in July 1919 to Catholic parents, who saw that she received a strict religious

education. Her father was a butcher and she nurtured ambitions to be a nurse, but was obliged to find work in a brewery and then as a domestic servant before she signed on for shift work at the Heinkel aircraft factory in Berlin. It was there that she became indoctrinated with Nazi ideology. She volunteered as a guard at Ravensbrück women's concentration camp in 1939 because it offered a higher wage and the status that came with authority and a uniform. As an unskilled factory worker she would have earned under 80 Reichsmarks a month, whereas as an unmarried camp overseer she would receive 185 Reichsmarks with all living expenses paid. It is known that she volunteered to work double shifts to supplement her income and because she enjoyed the 'work'.

At Ravensbrück, which held 26,700 prisoners by the war's end, she was one of almost 4,000 female guards. In total 132,000 women and children were imprisoned in the main camp and its satellite camps, of whom an estimated 92,000 died from overwork, disease, malnutrition, maltreatment, neglect and execution.

In October 1942, Braunsteiner was reassigned to Majdanek, where she exercised her new-found power as assistant warden by humiliating, brutalizing and whipping women prisoners for the slightest infractions of the rules. She was also feared and reviled for letting her savage German shepherd dog loose on those inmates to whom she took a dislike.

In 1944, she went back to Ravensbrück, where she was promoted to supervising warden, but she abandoned her post in July when word reached the camp that the Russians were approaching. She then went into hiding in Vienna, but she would have been present when the guards were ordered to erase as much 'evidence' as possible, which meant killing 130 infants and pregnant women.

Frustrated extradition attempts

After her eventual arrest in 1949, the Austrian authorities showed no inclination to make an example of her and after a perfunctory trial sentenced her to a token three years in prison for 'crimes of torture and abuse as well as the violation of human dignity' committed at Ravensbrück in 1941 and 1942. Her activities at Majdanek were not even considered. She was released the following year before serving her full sentence, given an assurance that she would not be prosecuted for her other crimes and granted amnesty.

Soon afterwards she met and married her American husband and they moved to Canada in October 1958 before eventually settling in New York, where she applied for citizenship.

To Lelyveld's astonishment there appeared to be no interest or urgency in extraditing 'Mrs Ryan', despite her having lied on her naturalization application regarding her conviction and imprisonment in Austria just 15 years earlier. But the INS (Immigration and Naturalization Service) were finally prodded into investigating the case by the American press, who wouldn't let go of the story. Seven long years later, they managed to trace a dozen surviving witnesses who were willing to testify to her crimes.

As soon as US government investigator Anthony DeVito collated the evidence he found himself unable to sleep. He was disturbed by nightmares night after night and by veiled threats to the life of his German wife by day, whose unlisted telephone number was apparently known only to employees of the INS. DeVito reported this to the FBI, but his complaint was not acted upon – he claimed they didn't interview him or his wife, although the threats constituted a federal offence.

Witnesses were intimidated and a high-price law firm specializing in immigration cases was assigned to defend Mrs Ryan. They were funded by an anonymous source which DeVito suspected was Odessa. The underground Nazi organization that had facilitated the 'rat lines' which enabled many war criminals to flee justice to South America, among them Dr Mengele and Adolf Eichmann, was thought by many to be a fiction created for *The Odessa File*, the recent bestseller by Frederick Forsyth. But Wiesenthal and other Nazi-hunters believed otherwise.

What had looked like an open and shut case to the young investigator now looked more like a conspiracy to save someone's embarrassment or integrity. More so when files including testimony from eight of the 12 witnesses mysteriously disappeared from a locked safe in the prosecutor's office, thereby seriously undermining the prosecution case.

On trial in Dusseldorf

When the Austrians provided proof of Braunsteiner's conviction she was allowed to cut a deal in which she voluntarily surrendered her citizenship in return for the right to stay and reapply for it in the future, when the media's interest in the case had died down. But when details of her crimes appeared in the newspapers, Americans were outraged that an alleged child-killer and sadistic murderer of women was living among them. The INS were forced to reopen the case and in 1971 they finally consented to extradite her after the West German government, who wanted her to stand trial with a group of Majdanek guards, provided 300 pages of documentation detailing her war-time activities in support of their application. However, she was perversely unrepentant and stubbornly refused to acknowledge her crimes, even when faced with the testimony of a dozen eyewitnesses to her cruelty.

On 22 April 1973, five weeks after her imprisonment in the Nassau County Jail, she wrote an embittered, self-pitying letter to her friends Hildegard and Renate Bex in Germany. It was dripping with sarcasm and hatred for those who had denied her liberty.

I cannot put into words how I miss my familiar home, my good-hearted Russ, and my loyal four-legged friends. For all of this I have to thank my dear friend J. And also the German government who see fit (under the enormous pressure and financial power of the most esteemed race) to judge me guilty after 34 years, and so to demand my extradition to convict me again, for everything that the German government designed and carried out back then … you don't even know what intrigue and dirty dealing has gone on in their treatment of my case, just to denounce me.

It is telling that she blames the 'German government' for the atrocities and mass murder in which she had actively and willingly participated. Two years later she was put on a flight to Düsseldorf and there she spent a further two years awaiting trial.

Midway through the trial BBC TV producer Tom Bower was 'on the trail of Nazi murderers' for a projected documentary. As his cameraman prepared to start filming Braunsteiner's arrival at Düsseldorf's courthouse, she suddenly appeared. Taking offence at being photographed she lashed out with her handbag and cracked the cameraman over the head.

Inside the courtroom, she affected an air of indifference by sitting hunched over a newspaper crossword. When she was requested to pay attention to the proceedings she asked: 'What do you want from me?'

Life imprisonment

All through her trial she refused to accept any responsibility for mass murder, portraying herself as a 'cog in the murder machine', as Bower described it. She had been a victim of the state as much as her victims, she claimed, and now she was the victim of a conspiracy to make Germans feel collective guilt for the crimes committed by the dictatorship.

But the court judged her to have been 'a committed and fanatical devotee of Nazism, ambitiously seeking promotion by murdering Jews'.

Over the next 20 years Bower interviewed dozens of former Nazis in Germany and South America, all of whom offered 'the same disarming pose of innocent obedience to orders, ignorance or helplessness about the fate of the Jews and other persecuted races', even though they came from a variety of backgrounds and possessed varying levels of intelligence. They appeared to have been subject to a collective neurosis. None expressed genuine remorse.

Bower's interviews revealed that both the male and female Nazi war criminals had been selected by the SS because of their 'devotion to Nazism' and a demonstrable lack of conscience and compassion. All of the concentration camp guards were 'groomed to prove their commitment' before being assigned to their duties, a process which was carefully controlled and monitored by their superiors. It was dishonest for them to claim that they had been innocent or unwilling participants. They were tested in successive 'murderous scenarios' and their approval of the brutal treatment meted out to those deemed 'unworthy of life' in euthanasia institutions and labour camps (two typical 'training facilities') was assessed. From there they would be sent to larger concentration camps where they were expected to participate in mass killings to prove their reliability. Failure to pass these tests was never punished, so Braunsteiner's argument that she would have been demoted or worse for refusing to take part was yet another lie.

> **MALE AND FEMALE NAZI WAR CRIMINALS WERE SELECTED BY THE SS BECAUSE OF THEIR 'DEVOTION TO NAZISM' AND A LACK OF CONSCIENCE AND COMPASSION**

In 1981, after the longest and most costly post-war German trial to date, Braunsteiner was convicted of the murder of 80 women and children, assisting in the murder of another 202 children and collaborating in the murder of another 1,000 prisoners, for which she was given two consecutive life sentences.

As a consequence of her successful extradition, New York prosecutor DeVito was provided with a list of 59 names of former Nazi war criminals living openly in the United States, who could now be held accountable for their crimes.

After serving 15 years of a life sentence, Hermine Braunsteiner was released on compassionate grounds, for reasons of declining health. Three years later, in 1999, she died at the age of 79. Her death went largely unreported, meriting only a footnote in the memoirs of that young reporter who had knocked on the door of the Brooklyn housewife who 'wouldn't hurt a fly'.

CHAPTER TEN

Living with the Reich

When SS officers were assigned to the concentration camps it was necessary to live on or near their posts, so they took their families along too. The conditions in which they lived were often relatively luxurious. For instance, the commandant of Ravensbrück and his family lived in a pretty, newly-built Swiss-style villa overlooking the camp. They were waited on by camp inmates who acted as servants and they hosted lavish dinner parties for local dignitaries and SS officers. Most of the wives were from the working-classes, so they rejoiced in, and sometimes abused, their newly-acquired status. A few, however, were less at ease with what was going on in the camps.

The children of the SS officers enjoyed idyllic and privileged childhoods as the crematorium worked to capacity. After the war, many of them were unable to believe that their kindly fathers had been responsible for the murders of millions of innocent people.

Minna Niemann

It is tempting to see history in black and white, to reduce historical personalities to the good, bad or indifferent and to view the choices that they made as clear and straightforward. But history was made by people who were prey to the same conflicting emotions that beset us today.

Minna Niemann despised the Nazi leaders and condemned them all as 'gangsters'. She expressed her contempt for the regime by dropping her *Mutterkreuz* (the medal they had awarded her for giving birth to a fourth child) in the bin along with the Christmas candle that the family were expected to place in a shrine dedicated to the Führer. This took the place of the traditional nativity scene.

WHEN EMACIATED CONCENTRATION CAMP INMATES CAME TO THE HOUSE TO FIT BUNK BEDS OR CARRY OUT REPAIRS, MINNA NIEMANN TALKED TO THEM AND FED THEM

When emaciated inmates from Sachsenhausen concentration camp came to the house to fit bunk beds for her children, or to carry out repairs, she talked to them and fed them, although it was expressly forbidden to do so. And yet Minna Niemann was married to an SS officer who was assigned to a succession of camps that became synonymous with inhuman cruelty.

When she met her future husband, Karl, in 1912, he had been a bank clerk; a conscientious, serious young man with modest ambitions, but it was to be eight years before they could marry. Karl went off to war in 1914 and did not return until six years later, as he had been captured and imprisoned by the French. They were impatient to make up for lost time, but had no illusions that married life would be anything but difficult and work hard to come by in a country beset with uncertainty and civil strife.

Shortly after the birth of their first child, Anna-Luise,

the German economy collapsed and Karl brought home his wages in a wheelbarrow. It was the era of hyperinflation and though the economy eventually stabilized, the respite was only temporary.

In 1929, the Wall Street Crash ushered in the years of high unemployment and violent street fighting as rival political factions fought for power all across Germany. It was in this climate of continual crisis that Karl joined the nascent NSDAP (National Socialist German Workers' Party). Hitler had predicted economic disaster in 1928, but at that point the NSDAP had attracted less than 3 per cent of the German vote. However, by the end of 1930 around four million people were unemployed and many were beginning to wonder if Hitler might perhaps be able to solve the economic problems he had predicted. In the general election of 1930 the number of NSDAP parliamentary representatives rose from 14 to 107 and the NSDAP became the second-largest party in the Reichstag.

Women of Minna's generation did not involve themselves in politics, or even make their views known outside the home. It was not their place. Minna objected to her husband's new associates and particularly the brutal methods they employed against those who disagreed with their extremist views, but she loved him and as his wife she had sworn to stand by him.

The couple now had three children to feed and clothe and Karl had been sacked from his job, so when he was offered another by a former school friend he gratefully accepted. That friend was Josef Spacil, then an SS officer on Himmler's staff. Spacil is believed to have been involved in the distribution of forged British banknotes at the end of the war and the hiding of stolen Nazi loot valued at 23 million gold marks. Minna loathed such men and could not hide her feelings, but she knew it was futile to try to dissuade her husband from associating with them.

'Can't you smell the flesh?'

Karl's new role required the family to move to Bavaria, where he became the auditor for an SS office at Dachau. Opened in 1933, it was the first concentration camp and had been used initially to imprison political opponents of the regime. However, by 1936, when Karl Niemann reported for duty, it was being used to incarcerate Jehovah's Witnesses, homosexuals and minorities (that is, Jews) who had been criminalized by the infamous Nuremberg Laws, which had been passed the previous year.

Minna could do little but insist on giving birth to the second of her three sons in the next town so the name of Dachau would not be on his birth certificate. Against her wishes the boy was named Eckart Josef, after his father's benefactor and friend.

His middle name was Adolf and he grew up to tell his own children that their grandfather was 'a true Nazi. He believed in Hitler until he found out all the bad things. He was a disappointed man.'

Even before the first mass extermination of prisoners at the death camps, women of Minna's intelligence and awareness knew that such places were forced labour camps and not mere prisons. Although they didn't talk about it, the purpose of the camp and its brutal regime was common knowledge among the SS wives with whom Minna socialized during picnics in the countryside and day trips to the Alps.

Two years later Karl was reassigned to the capital and promoted to business manager for the SS. His duties involved inspections of all the camps, during which he was to evaluate the productivity of their slave labour factories. Minna, however, refused to remain impassive and when she had the chance to express her contempt for the regime in her own way, she seized upon it. It seems that she was not alone in treating some of the inmates humanely.

Perhaps some of what she said finally impressed her husband, for late in the war he would bring home a former prisoner who was then working for him to share their Sunday lunch. It later transpired, from testimony given at Karl's post-war tribunal, that he had struck deals with his SS colleagues for the release of a number of inmates, although he would persist in his assertion that he had not known of the mass exterminations.

Their second son Eckart was 11 years old when he heard his mother say to Karl, as they watched the billowing smoke rising from the chimneys of the crematoria at Dachau: 'You know what they are doing there? They're killing the Jews and burning the bodies.'

'No, they wouldn't do that,' was his father's reply.

But his mother would not let it go.

'Yes, they would, can't you smell the flesh?'

Karl spent three years in internment at the end of the war and returned to their first home in Hamelin to find his wife waiting patiently as she had done when he had returned from the First World War, only this time there were changes. She had framed the photo of their eldest son Dieter, who had been killed in action at the age of 19 while serving as a member of a tank crew, but the SS flashes on his black uniform had been crudely erased with a pen. She wanted to remember their boy, not the regime for which he had sacrificed his life in vain.

Brigitte Hoess

For most of her life Washington fashion model Brigitte Hoess suffered from splitting migraines, which began the evening the Allies came to arrest her father, Rudolf, the commandant of Auschwitz. It was a chilly early spring day in March 1946 and she was then 13 years old. The headaches finally eased a few years before her hair turned white in her early seventies, but returned in December 2010, on the day she reluctantly agreed to talk about her past and her parents. She has described her father as 'the nicest man in the world', so it was painful to attempt to reconcile that image with his admission that he supervised the murder of over three million people.

Brigitte (born Inge-Brigitt in 18 August 1933) was not ashamed of her father or her mother who had stood by him and had kept an unframed photograph above her bed of her parents taken on their wedding day, 17 August 1929, a year after Rudolf had been released from prison after serving four years for the brutal murder of a school-teacher in Mecklenburg. He was then a member of the Freikorps, a far-right paramilitary group that was to form the core of the Brownshirts or SA (Sturmabteilung).

Rudolf Hoess and Hedwig Hensel had met on a farm near the Baltic Sea while both were members of the Artaman League, a back-to-the-land movement with extreme nation-alist sympathies. While he was a member of the League Hoess came under the influence of Heinrich Himmler, eventually joining the SS in April 1934 to serve the man he admired more than Hitler.

By the time Hoess had been assigned to Auschwitz he had proved himself a loyal and obedient functionary at Dachau (December 1934–38) where he served as a Blockführer (barracks leader) and at Sachsenhausen (1938–1940), where he acted as adjutant to the commandant.

MAINLY FROM WORKING-CLASS BACKGROUNDS, THE NAZI WOMEN, ENJOYED HIGHER SOCIAL STATUS BY BEING THE WIVES OF SS MEN

On 1 May 1940 Himmler appointed him as commandant of a new prison camp in western Poland, where the 'final solution of the Jewish question' was to be implemented. Hoess arrived with his heavily pregnant wife and four children; two girls and two boys. Brigitte, the middle of his three daughters, was then seven.

The family moved into the camp 'villa', a moderately large two-storey house in secluded grounds adjacent to the crematorium, where Hoess experimented with Zyklon B, an industrial pesticide derivative which was to prove the most economical and efficient method of murder. Meanwhile Hedwig furnished the villa with tapestries and paintings stolen from prisoners. She also ordered the construction of a large greenhouse stocked with exotic plants and a pool for their freshwater fish. In summer, she took the children to swim in the Sola river and in winter they travelled to the surrounding snowbound villages by sled.

Family life in the camp

The Nazi women, who were mainly from working-class backgrounds, soon discovered that they were automatically elevated to a higher social status by being the wives of SS men. They enjoyed an upper middle class or professional lifestyle without having the means to finance it. Everything was paid for and laid on for them.

Their privileged lives included being waited on by servants who had been spared from the slave-labour details and the gas chambers to serve their Aryan masters. Hedwig hosted lavish dinner parties for local dignitaries and SS officers, while the children were entertained, bathed, clothed or fed by two elderly female prisoners, both Jehovah's Witnesses, who acted as unpaid nannies. Prisoners also supplied the children with handmade toys and small pets such as lizards and turtles, caught in the nearby woods and fields, presumably in the faint hope of receiving lenient treatment. The girls had their own ponies and the older boys rode horses. The only time they were made aware that there was something unpleasant in their sham paradise was the day they were caught playing 'Kapo and Prisoner' in the garden. (A Kapo was a trusted prisoner who had been assigned supervisory or administrative duties. Kapos could be as brutal as the guards themselves.) Their father flew into a rage and tore off the coloured triangles that they had stuck to their clothes.

Although the Hoess children were restricted to playing in the house and garden, there were many other German families in the area whose children had a freer run of the town and its surroundings, so many in fact that in the summer of 1944 the SS leadership actively discouraged more families from moving to Auschwitz. There was a large contingent from Dachau, including the son and daughter of Karl Fritzch, the first Auschwitz camp compound leader, whose children had been born in the SS settlement outside Munich and had attended the local SS nursery. Relocating from the city to private accommodation near the camp appealed to the wives of SS men for a number of reasons. Not only were they close to their husbands, but they felt their children were safer from Allied air raids. The men too were more comfortable living away from the camp in a residential area than in a crowded barracks and were able to distance themselves from the routine brutality by returning to the artificial stability of their families. Some routinely came home for lunch as if they had been working in a regular job, although Hoess admitted that their uniforms stank of decay and smoke that 'permeated the entire area'.

Happy days for some

While the Hoess children played in a sandpit or in the paddling pool in the walled garden, emaciated prisoners worked just yards away in their familiar striped uniforms. Some were even admitted to the house to work as cooks, nannies, seamstresses and cleaners. Having enjoyed an idyllic childhood, Brigitte predictably shared her mother's impression of their days in Poland as being like 'paradise' and recalled these poor specimens of humanity as 'always very happy'. She claimed that her mother had given food to some of their servants, who called her 'The Angel of Auschwitz'. No such testimony was recorded and no verification of this claim is known to exist.

One of their gardeners, Stanislaw Dubiel, later reported a conversation in which he heard Frau Hoess express her hope that all the Jews would be wiped off the face of the earth. She was then heard to refer to her husband as the 'special commissioner for the extermination of Jews in Europe'. Hoess later confessed to having ignored his own order not to discuss Nazi policy regarding the Jews with his family.

The main functions of the camp, its gas chambers and crematoria, were common knowledge among the families of the guards and the staff. Against the commandant's explicit orders, his men would invite their wives, mistresses and local girls to tour the camp while boasting of their power over the prisoners. Birkenau camp compound leader Johann Schwarzhuber forced Soviet prisoners to dance for the amusement of his family, who watched from the other side of the barbed wire fence, and the children of SS men were permitted to walk freely around the compound until Hoess prohibited it in July 1943.

As Nikolaus Wachsmann observes in *KL: A History of the Nazi Concentration Camps*, these women

> stood behind the camps and condoned their husband's crimes, tacitly or openly. By performing their role as SS wives and creating a semblance of normality at the *anus mundi* (arse of the world), these women became complicit in the atrocities.

They did not, of course, allow such notions to spoil their luxurious lifestyles. As the widow of the former Plaszow commandant Amon Goeth noted: 'My Goeth was the King and I was the Queen. Who wouldn't have traded places with us?'

Betrays husband

Hedwig Hoess certainly entertained no qualms. She chose to remain in the villa at Auschwitz after her husband was transferred to the SS Main Economic and Administrative Office at Oranienburg in late 1943, where SS couriers regularly deposited huge quantities of valuables looted from prisoners. According to Brigitte, her mother was: 'Unbelievable, wonderful ... the nicest person in the world.'

But her mother too had secrets. On learning that her husband had been engaged in an affair with a political prisoner, Eleanor Hodys, and that Hodys had had an abortion, Hedwig determined to have her revenge by engaging in an affair with their German cook, Karola Bohnera. Even after their relationship was discovered she continued to see him in defiance of her husband.

It was Hedwig who ultimately betrayed her husband to the Allies, informing them of his hiding place and the false name that he was using at the time, although she told her family that it was her brother Fritz who had denounced him.

New life in the US

After the war Brigitte found an American husband who promised not to probe into her past and a Jewish employer who overlooked her background out of simple 'humanity', though she herself refused to be so magnanimous, dismissing the period in pathetically inadequate terms as 'sad' and pleading to be allowed to leave such horrors in the past. 'It was such a long time ago ... I never talk about it ... It is best not to remember those things.'

It is hard to believe her assertion that she was the only child in the family not to have shown any curiosity about the barbed wire fences and watchtowers that she could see from her bedroom window. She remembered watching the smoke rising from the crematorium, but insisted that she never asked what was happening on the other side of the garden wall.

Her brother Hans-Jurgen did not share her sentimental memories of their childhood. He remembered the pungent stench of the smoke from the crematorium and told his wife it had been 'a terrible time'. His wife, Irene Alba, would live to confirm that Hedwig had known of the gas chambers, the beatings, the indiscriminate executions and the random brutality. Brigitte kept a copy of her father's

HANS-JURGEN DID NOT SHARE HER SENTIMENTAL MEMORIES OF THEIR CHILDHOOD. HE REMEMBERED THE PUNGENT STENCH OF THE CREMATORIUM

autobiography in her bedroom but struggled to read it. 'There must have been two sides to him. The one that I knew and then another,' she told writer Thomas Harding.

She only agreed to be interviewed after extracting a promise from Harding, the grand-nephew of the British officer (a German Jewish émigré) who had arrested her father, that her married name and other identifying details be withheld, for despite insisting that she had nothing to be ashamed of she had kept her real identity a secret, even from her own family. She saw herself as a 'victim' after her mother and siblings found themselves shunned by their fellow Germans after the war and were forced to flee to Spain, where she became a fashion model.

Holocaust denial

She continued to act the part of a persecuted Nazi apologist even after moving into a $650,000 home in Washington, Virginia with her American husband. Her irrational fear of retribution from 'crazy people' who might set fire to her house 'or shoot somebody' found expression also in her denial of her father's involvement in genocide. 'How can there be so many survivors if so many had been killed?' she asked, having adopted one of the rehearsed responses trotted out at every opportunity by Holocaust deniers.

When confronted with her father's damning confession she dismissed it as having been extracted 'under torture'.

Had the Jewish soldiers who tracked her father down given in to their own lust for vengeance he would not have survived to take the stand at Nuremberg, where his chilling testimony provided a first-hand account of mass murder on an industrial scale. It condemned him to a second trial by the Poles, who found him guilty of complicity in the murder of more than a million Jews as well as hundreds of thousands of political prisoners, Catholics, Gypsies and other 'enemies of the state'.

Admission of guilt

According to the Auschwitz museum, of the '1.3 million or more people' deported to Auschwitz-Birkenau 232,000 were children. Only 700 of these remained alive when the camp was liberated by the Russians on 27 January 1945. Many had been subjected to sadistic 'medical' experiments by the notorious camp physician Dr Mengele, who evaded justice by fleeing to South America.

Rudolf Hoess was not so fortunate. He was executed on 16 April 1947, on the site where he had presided over the death and suffering of so many innocent people that the true number will probably never be known. Shortly before he was hanged, he dictated a message to the State Prosecutor in which he made an admission of guilt and acknowledged his responsibility.

My conscience compels me to make the following declaration. In the solitude of my prison cell, I have come to the bitter recognition that I have sinned gravely against humanity. As commandant of Auschwitz, I was responsible for carrying out part of the cruel plans of the 'Third Reich' for human destruction. In so doing I have inflicted terrible wounds on humanity. I caused unspeakable suffering for the Polish people in particular. I am to pay for this with my life. May the Lord God forgive one day what I have done.

Only Brigitte's nephew, Rainer, Rudolf's grandson, has had the courage to face his family's past and now lectures to schoolchildren on the evils of totalitarianism. 'If I knew where he was buried,' Rainer says of his infamous grandfather, 'I would piss on his grave.'

Ravensbrück wives

Anna Koegel

Hoess was not the only commandant to live with his family in such close proximity to a camp. Max Koegel, commandant of Ravensbrück concentration camp for women from January 1940 to August 1942, and his successor Fritz Suhren, commandant from August 1942 until April 1945, both brought their wives to live in the Swiss-style villa overlooking the compound.

Anna Koegel (née Jilecek), a thickset, stern-faced, officious and overbearing woman, married her husband when he was an SS adjutant at Dachau. She wholeheartedly approved of his brutal treatment of the Jewish inmates which she felt they deserved, which was probably something to do with having been prevented from pursuing her career as a singer after her father's Jewish employer had been forced to make him redundant. She had found work as a doctor's receptionist, then as a kindergarten teacher and finally as a waitress before she met Max Koegel, a former shop owner and divorcee.

Nursing a grievance against all Jews for frustrating her career, she verbally abused the prisoners who were compelled to work in the SS beauty salon, taking a particular pleasure in having them dye her jet-black hair without the protection of gloves, a process which was painful for the prisoners who had open cuts and sores from ill treatment and malnutrition.

The couple had no children. After the war, Max committed suicide rather than face trial, leaving his wife free to remarry.

Elfriede Suhren

Elfriede Suhren (née Bruns) had a very different personality. A quiet unassuming woman, she brought her four children to live at the villa on the mound at Ravensbrück in August 1942 and settled down to a life of routine domesticity, hosting cocktail parties for her husband's staff and playing the role of the ideal SS wife. She was blonde, slim and expressed no particular opinion on anything other than the colour of the curtains or her dislike for his collection of Hummel figurines and the mounted animal heads that stared down glassy-eyed from the walls of the study. (Based on the sketches of idealized little children by Sister Maria Innocentia Hummel and manufactured by Franz Goebel, Hummel porcelain figurines were very popular in Germany at the time. It is difficult to reconcile Suhren's fondness for these charming figures with his total disregard for the lives of hundreds of children in his camp, many of whom were starved, inhumanely treated or even murdered.)

Fritz Suhren was an early convert to National Socialism (having joined the Party in 1928) and was eager to demonstrate his initiative by ordering the construction of a crematorium which could incinerate up to 150 bodies a day. He was also a sadist who habitually prolonged executions by any means he could devise and who implemented a policy at Ravensbrück of working prisoners to death to save the trouble of executing them. But he too had his principles, for he apparently objected to supplying inmates for medical experiments on the grounds that they were political prisoners. After the war, Elfriede naively petitioned former prisoners to testify on his behalf at his trial before a French tribunal, but they all refused. He was convicted and executed.

A young woman from the Sudetenland region of Czechoslovakia decorates a portrait of Hitler with swastika flags in 1938. Shortly after this propaganda photo was first published, the Germans marched into the Sudetenland.

Getty

Adolf Hitler consoles a woman widowed by the Munich Beer Hall Putsch of 1923, the Nazis' cack-handed attempt to seize power in Germany, but a failure the Nazis never stopped making political capital out of. Each year – this photograph was taken in 1935 – they commemorated the event with greater and greater ceremony, including a roll-call of the dead 'martyrs' with their widows in attendance. Although the facts are murky, it seems as if Hitler probably ran away that day in 1923, but this possibility was never mentioned in what became a more and more grandiose myth-building exercise.

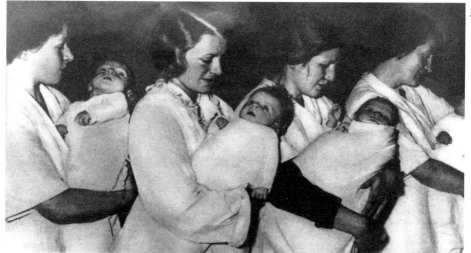

German women hold babies at a *Lebensborn* birth clinic, part of Heinrich Himmler's warped vision for producing a new elite of blond, blue-eyed children for the '1,000-year Reich'. The aim was to test out theories of eugenics using 'Aryan' women and specially selected SS men. With clinics in Germany, Austria, Norway and other parts of Hitler's short-lived empire, lots of money was spent, but the children produced ended up being tragically damaged for the rest of their lives.

The parade of German Women gymnasts at the Berlin Olympics in 1936. The Olympic Games had been agreed to by a previous regime, the Weimar government, and inherited by the Nazis, who did not share the movement's high-minded ideals about internationalism, or the desirability of peaceful co-existence between nations. In fact, the very opposite. Like all authoritarians, the Nazis preferred to portray their athletes, not as individuals, but as beautiful, well-maintained robots that obediently carried out their bidding, performing for the state without ever expressing an opinion of any kind.

Princess Stephanie von Hohenlohe-Waldenburg-Schillingfürst was only 5ft 5in; she took up less space than her name in lights. And truly nobody ever forgot the woman who smoked Havana cigars, which she lit by striking matches on the sole of her shoe. The princess was the archetypal femme fatale and temptress showered with gifts by wealthy suitors. On behalf of her paymasters the Nazis, she persuaded Lord Rothermere to support them with his UK newspapers, and she had an affair with Hitler's personal adjutant, Fritz Wiedemann. Few could resist her charms, including Hitler.

Mothering Sunday, 1942, and Magda Goebbels hands out the Mother's Cross of Honour to a succession of German Mother Hubbards who had so many children they didn't know what to do. Mothers with eight or more kids earned the gold version; six or seven kids merited silver; and four or five meant bronze. A Gold Cross with diamonds was proposed for those who produced more than twelve offspring. Goebbels (photographed here with her daughter Holde) was given the title 'First Mother of the Reich' by Hitler just prior to his suicide and not long before her own six young kids were put to death at her insistence in the bunker.

Getty

Women hang freshly laundered Nazi banners out to dry. These women were a tiny part of the myth-making machinery of Germany. As Hitler said, 'A powerful insignia alone can spark interest in a political movement,' and that's why the Nazi emblems of power were displayed everywhere, giving the Nazis the veneer of invincibility. But in this case, as so often, the men took the glory while the women did the hard work behind the scenes.

Getty

The women of Styria (then in Nazi-occupied Austria) descend on Nuremberg in traditional *Dirndls* for the 1938 Nuremberg Rally. It was a big day out for them, but where they had come from – in what was now called the Ostmark by the Nazis – waves of repression had begun against the Jews and all those who resisted the Nazis.

In 1943, Stella Kuebler and her parents were arrested by the Nazis and tortured. In order to avoid deportation, she agreed to become a 'catcher' for the Gestapo, hunting down Jews hiding as non-Jews (known as 'U-Boats' because they were submerged) in Berlin. She handed over between 600 and 3,000 victims, many of whom suffered terrible fates. No wonder her nickname among the Nazis was 'blonde poison'.

Nicknamed 'Axis Sally' and born Mildred Elizabeth Sisk in Portland, Maine, Mildred Gillars hosted a radio show for German state radio called *Home Sweet Home*, designed to make members of the US Forces in Europe insecure about their sweethearts at home, their mission in Europe, and their prospects after the war. In *GI's Letter-box* and *Medical Reports*, Gillars used detailed information about wounded and captured US airmen to spread fear and alarm among their families back home. She was later charged with treason.

Adolf Hitler described film-maker Leni Riefenstahl as the perfect German woman. In 1934, she directed a despicable masterpiece called *Triumph of the Will*, which used revolutionary new techniques to glorify the Nazis and lend them a mythic quality. Later, she filmed the 1936 Berlin Olympics, pioneering many new camera techniques. By the time, Riefenstahl arrived in New York in 1938 to promote her film *Olympia*, news of the *Kristallnacht* pogroms had reached the US and no studio boss in Hollywood would let her in through the door, with the exception of Walt Disney. Here she is pictured trying to put a brave face on affairs during her return journey to Germany aboard the ocean liner *Hansa*.

Nuremberg Rally in 1937: Zeppelin Field. 'I am beginning to comprehend,' wrote William L. Shirer, a major critic of the Third Reich, after a visit to Germany, 'some of the reasons for Hitler's astounding success… he is restoring pageantry and color and mysticism to the drab lives of 20th Century Germans.' Seduced by the power of Hitler, millions of German women were hypnotized, even aroused, by the sight and sound of Nazi spectacle. Films of Hitler at the Nuremberg Rallies were edited to emphasize the ecstatic reaction of his audiences (and, in particular, the young women). Nothing was left to chance in promoting the myth of the Führer.

CHAPTER ELEVEN

Growing Up Under Hitler

In the years following the Nazi Party's rise to power, everyone was expected to accede to the Party's demands. For instance, German public employees had to give the 'Heil Hitler' salute and anyone who failed to conform would be punished. The Party even told the German people what to eat for Sunday lunch. It was in this climate of repression and intimidation that the persecution of the Jews began. Few loyal citizens wanted to interfere, many remaining inside their homes.

Children were affected too. Schools were made to adopt the Nazi curriculum and membership of the Hitler Youth was mandatory after 1936. Those who refused to join faced a variety of consequences. The girls' version, the BDM (Bund Deutscher Mädel), was a voluntary organization until 1939, but many girls joined before then, often in defiance of their parents.

It was easy for a child like Marianne Gartner to believe the Nazi lies and constant propaganda and to be instilled with patriotic fervour. But as the war went on and she encountered scenes of horror at every turn she could no longer deny the evidence of her own eyes. In the end the words of an ineffectual and broken Führer rang hollow in her ears.

Marianne Gartner

Although the Nazis sought to dominate and control the population, ordinary Germans continued to struggle with the trials of daily life much as they had before Hitler took power.

In the summer of 1936, when all of Germany seemed to be in a state of eager excitement in anticipation of the Berlin Olympics, ten-year-old Marianne Gartner was experiencing the turmoil of her parents' failing marriage. The innocence of her childhood and the peace of her home had been shattered by ugly, heated arguments. They pursued her in her sleep, spawning nightmares from which she would awake screaming, bringing her mother to stroke away the fear and reassure her that it had only been a dream.

But Marianne was no longer a child. She had been prematurely awoken to adulthood by the trauma of her parents' constant quarrelling and now saw them as far from the perfect, reassuring presence that had been a feature of her early life. At the same time, she was becoming aware that the real world was not the familiar, friendly place it had once appeared to be.

To begin with there was the voice. That intrusive disembodied guttural voice that boomed out of the wireless in the living room, 'sending little shivers down my spine'. Although Marianne had no idea what Hitler was saying, he sounded like a cross between a stern schoolmaster and 'an angry prophet'. And he clearly provoked the other tenants of their apartment building to bicker and squabble instead of greeting each other amicably as they used to do.

Learning to be a Nazi

At school there were new rules, new books, new songs to learn and an entirely new syllabus with an emphasis on sport. Pupils and teachers alike had to greet each other with the 'Heil Hitler' salute. Those who refused, like the family physician, were quietly removed from public life. The kind doctor no longer came in the middle of the night when Marianne was ill. Her parents didn't offer an explanation but simply looked embarrassed, as if they had been discovered doing something they should be ashamed of.

About the same time, her father joined the Party under much protest, which he voiced only at home. He also acquired a uniform and a Party badge was pinned to the lapel of the smart worsted suit he wore to work as sales director of a prosperous steel company.

The Olympics proved a welcome distraction from Marianne's unhappy home life, more so since her class was to take part in the Youth Pageant which followed the opening ceremony. In her words, 'The world had come to Berlin', and this gave her the first glimpse of people with dark or yellow skin wearing turbans, kimonos and traditional costumes, while all around came the sound of exotic, unfamiliar languages.

Before a crowd of 100,000 onlookers Marianne's class performed their graceful dance routine to the strains of piped music, in perfect synchronization with hundreds of Berlin's school children in starched white uniforms. More than once she glanced over at the grandstand where the Führer was watching. He seemed to have his eyes on her, but later many girls would say the same.

Hitler Youth

Two weeks later, after the games had finished and the decorations and flags were packed away, she was confronted with harsh reality. Her parents were to be divorced and would be sending her away to an institution for orphans and the daughters of broken homes. There she would languish for five years, cycling to a school where her classmates shunned her because she lived in an orphanage and wore its drab, musty-smelling uniform. She would see her parents separately at the weekends and learned to live with the fact that she would not be invited to her classmates' birthday parties because she had no real home or family. But in retrospect she realized that the girls' home was a refuge from the world outside, a world now dominated by martial music, speeches, banners and political indoctrination.

However, by the spring of 1938 even the gentle matron, who had gleefully distributed the official Party newspaper for use as toilet paper, had to concede to the dictates of the school and Party officials and allow her girls to join the BDM.

Outbreak of war

Marianne took the oath on Hitler's birthday with no thought other than the appealing prospect of participating in games and other activities that would take her away from the home and from school. But very soon she found herself marching in step, drilling like a toy soldier for what seemed like hours on end and being lectured on the dogma of National Socialism.

The following year she greeted the outbreak of war with indifference, noting only the increased military

> **MARIANNE TOOK THE OATH BUT SOON FOUND HERSELF MARCHING IN STEP, DRILLING LIKE A TOY SOLDIER AND BEING LECTURED ON NATIONAL SOCIALISM**

presence at the local barracks and the front-line trains streaming out of Potsdam station decorated with the painted slogan: 'Wheels must turn for victory.'

Other than that, all seemed normal in the early days of the war before the Allied air raids. Marianne took part in the compulsory Winter Aid street collections, rattling her tin can at every passer-by and taking bets with the other children on who would fill their can first. But she and her classmates regarded the exercise as a waste of good playing time and were equally resentful at having to join the periodic door-to-door collections for rags, bones, waste paper, scrap metal and even combed-out hair. In spring and summer there were the harvests of strawberries and potatoes to supplement the war economy and the obligatory Eintopf (one pot), a meatless stew which replaced the traditional Sunday lunch, the money saved being donated to Winter Aid, a Nazi charity.

It all seemed worthy to a young girl in the midst of the patriotic fever generated by those early victories until she read a letter from an aunt who lived in São Paulo, Brazil, sympathizing with her niece and her divorced sister, who now lived under a dictatorship. Her mother tore the letter to pieces, fearing that someone might find it and report the contents to the Gestapo.

Aristocratic lodgings

After spending five years in the girls' home, Marianne was sent to live with the sons and daughters of high-ranking Wehrmacht officers, landowners and diplomats who were boarding in the palatial residence of a titled family overlooking Sanssouci Park in a wealthy suburb of Potsdam. As a member of the BDM, the first thing she noticed was the conspicuous absence of framed portraits of the Führer. Instead the walls of the villa were hung with formal paintings of Bismarck, the former Kaiser and officers of the old school. The baron was a lieutenant colonel and a staff officer who would later take a prominent role in the July plot to assassinate Hitler.

Although Marianne had been offered a room in the villa in exchange for tutoring one of the daughters, she was made to feel like a servant whose presence was only tolerated because of her usefulness. The baroness belittled her at every opportunity but she came to admire the baron, who gave them all a daily situation report on the fighting on the Eastern Front, with its succession of tactical withdrawals.

He was perfectly frank about the ferocity of the Russian winter and the desperate plight of the besieged Sixth Army at Stalingrad. Such news was greeted with stoicism and stubborn defiance by Party loyalists among the boarders and the domestic staff but, as Marianne admitted, even someone as poor at arithmetic as herself could calculate that the winter woollens they were knitting would not reach their frostbitten and snowbound troops until well after the spring thaw.

An unauthorized date with a young aristocratic officer led to her expulsion from the villa, which Marianne did not attribute to the breach of propriety but rather to the fact that he had been reserved for the baroness's daughter. Her next home was to challenge all that had been instilled in her by the BDM, for she was to be boarding in the house of a Jew.

Questions Nazism

Her father had found her the room in the Benjamin home because it was the only respectable house he could find. Herr Benjamin, a city banker, had been taken away a year earlier and had not been seen since. However, his wife was an Aryan and so was allowed to keep their house, a luxury villa in Potsdam which she shared with their three teenaged children, who were officially *Halbjuden* (half-Jews) or *Mischlinge* (of mixed blood).

But their estate and savings had been seized, leaving them with no income, so they reluctantly welcomed Marianne into their home as a paying guest. They were grateful for her food coupons, which would supplement their meagre rations, but unable to hide their anxiety from her, nor their anger at what was happening to the less fortunate members of their race.

For the first time, Marianne was forced to confront the lies and slurs that had been hammered into her by her Gruppenführer in the BDM, her schoolteachers and the incessant propaganda with which the Reich's citizens had been force-fed on a daily basis for the past five years. She recalled seeing the aftermath of *Kristallnacht*, when the SA thugs had smashed Jewish-owned shops and businesses, beaten their owners and burned synagogues to the ground while the police refused to intervene and the population either looked on approvingly or remained inside their homes.

I was conscious all of a sudden of a twinge of guilt for having allowed my sunflower philosophy to ignore or doubt the truth of rumours ... But then, I thought, how many people are ready to take rumours at face value, particularly if they stretch the imagination to its limits.

Despite all the propaganda, the regime could not stifle the awakening curiosity of an adolescent who began questioning and trying to rationalize everything she had been taught. That Christmas, as Marianne sat in church listening to the minister preach his sermon, it occurred to her that congregations in Russia, Britain and western Europe were all petitioning their God for victory – the same God who, she had been taught, never took sides, did not restore peace between warring nations and did not award victory to the side which prayed the hardest.

Stalingrad defeat

Then in February 1943 came the news that Stalingrad had fallen after a five-month siege, during which an estimated 300,000 German soldiers and their allies were killed, starved to death or frozen as the temperature plummeted to minus 30 degrees. In addition, 90,000 officers and men of the once undefeated Sixth Army had surrendered to the Red Army. Hitler had assured his commanders that the Soviet forces had been decimated by Stalin's purges of their officers and would therefore be unable to offer serious resistance, but his prediction was far from the truth.

Goebbels attempted to portray one of the worst defeats in German military history as a glorious sacrifice and then declared 'total war'; elderly men were conscripted into the *Volkssturm* (People's Militia) and women were drafted into the munitions factories or deployed to defence units. Only mothers with young children were exempt. Three days of national mourning saw bars, cafes, cinemas and other places of public entertainment close, along with many shops and restaurants. The true cost of Hitler's obdurate 'no retreat' policy was only apparent the following spring, when lists of the dead were still appearing in the German newspapers.

The Benjamin family enjoyed a brief period of *Schadenfreude* during which they prayed that the end of the war and their ordeal would now soon come, but the two boys were sent to labour camps and their mother and sister were forced out of their home when Party officials occupied the villa for use as offices. Marianne was again homeless, but because she was a loyal Party member she soon found herself billeted in luxurious surroundings.

War sacrifices

The smart white villa on the banks of the Heiligensee belonged to a wealthy childless couple who evidently lavished all their affection on their art collection and antiques. They were relieved to have the daughter of a prominent businessman as their lodger, someone who would know how to behave in their private museum, as opposed to the German refugees from the eastern provinces whom Potsdam's residents were now obliged to house if they had a spare room or two.

'I don't want to sound like a snob,' Herr Mangert, the householder, explained as he proudly showed Marianne and her father around the opulently furnished rooms, 'but I hear that most of them are really no more than peasants.'

Marianne was asked to keep to her room, a converted attic, and make herself as unobtrusive as possible. She was also discouraged from cooking as the housekeeper was apparently 'jealous of her kitchen'.

While their fellow Berliners would 'reap the whirl-wind' promised by RAF commander Sir Arthur 'Bomber' Harris and endured the increasing privations and sacrifices demanded of them by the war, the Mangerts continued to live their isolated, self-centred lives, their 'skin-deep smiles' betraying the impression that for them charity was no more 'than a Christian catch-phrase'.

While her reluctant hosts ate well, Marianne survived as most Berliners did that year on 'thin soup', cabbage, fried potatoes, skimmed milk pudding and 'mean sandwiches'. She grew tired and listless, neglecting the athletic training with which she had made a name for herself in the BDM and by which she had compensated for her poor academic grades. 'The Reich's fitness-orientated policies,' she later wrote, 'had been rigidly enforced in schools for years, inevitably at the expense of academic subjects.'

Predictably, she failed to graduate and was offered the option to repeat the year, something for which she could summon no enthusiasm, but at least she would be safer at school.

Father's expulsion

In the meantime, she was ordered to report for work on a farm where she would be looking after small children, helping in the house and working in the fields. A six-week compulsory working holiday, as she saw it. It could have been worse. She might have remained in the city where nightly air raids were making life hell for the general population; with the exception of the Mangerts, who had built their own private underground shelter in their back garden, wired with electricity and furnished with a safe, a Schnapps cabinet and a priceless oil painting.

> **THE MANGERTS HAD BUILT THEIR OWN UNDERGROUND SHELTER IN THE BACK GARDEN, FURNISHED WITH A SAFE, SCHNAPPS CABINET AND PRICELESS OIL PAINTING**

Her stint at the farm proved demanding but not unpleasant, as the farmer and his family were friendly and Marianne had been billeted there with a former school friend, an easygoing girl with a sharp sense of humour. The only sour note was sounded when the farmer's wife, Frau Hansen, informed their guests over their first evening meal – a steaming meat stew of the kind that had not been seen in the city for months – that their eldest son had been killed at Stalingrad.

Although they had sacrificed a son, the Hansens were no supporters of the regime. National Socialism had not improved their lives one bit. Being part of a self-reliant, self-contained rural community, they resented having to satisfy production quotas, comply with regulations and be supervised and dictated to by ignorant officials who took advantage of their authority to line their own pockets. 'Out here, we have our own government,' Herr Hansen told the girls one evening. 'We've had it for generations. Our soil, our livestock needs us and we need them, no matter what bloke or political party runs the country.'

Up to this point, Marianne had viewed her many upheavals and trials as the misfortunes of living in a country at war, but on her return to Berlin at the end of the summer she learned what living in a dictatorship meant. Her father had been expelled from the Party for making derogatory remarks about the *Goldfasane* (Golden Pheasants or Nazi 'big shots'; so called because of their light brown uniforms and golden insignia), and was being posted to Warsaw to run a steel mill manned by Polish and Russian slave workers. He described it to her on their last meeting as a 'suicide mission', for the Polish underground were becoming more daring as the Russians moved closer to the capital. Father and daughter said their goodbyes, believing that it might be their last.

Berlin in flames

That term Marianne and her classmates were given their Abitur certificate regardless of their grades and dismissed from school six months early. All pupils over the age of 17 were needed for war service. After a brief spell, Marianne was sent to work in a kindergarten in the Oder-Neisse region, on the border between Germany and Poland, after which she was instructed to report to a small town west of Posen to work for Organization Todt, the state construction organization.

When she finally returned to Berlin in February 1945, after the Russians had overrun Posen, she found much of the city in flames and the besieged citizens scurrying for cover. Though her father's home had been reduced to rubble the year before and her grandmother's house was now a blackened shell, her mother's apartment block had miraculously survived the relentless day and night air assaults.

Her experiences and the sights she had witnessed on her harrowing journey home had made a profound and lasting impression.

I no longer saw in death the final serenity of old age which knows its time has come, nor the nobility and decorum of *Vaterlandstod* (death for the Fatherland) as it had been glorified in school and Hitler Youth books, with no mention of its hideousness, its futility or its anguish.

The survivors had lost most of their possessions as well as their loved ones, friends and neighbours. They lived in perpetual darkness even during the day for almost all of the windows in the few buildings that were deemed inhabitable were now boarded up. Life was lived underground in the overcrowded airless cellars and shelters. Gas, water and electricity supplies were disrupted and the citizens of 'the city of light' were now scavenging for food and clothing. It was clear to all that the war was lost 'and that only the magnitude and the depth of the suffering still to come remained unknown'.

GOING OUT BECAME PERILOUS AND GIRLS LIKE MARIANNE RISKED THEIR LIVES IN THE CROSSFIRE FOR A LOAF OF BREAD. NO ONE WAS BAKING FRESH BREAD

Hitler's final broadcasts

From open windows, street cafes and the comforting dark of the few cinemas that remained open in defiance of the encroaching storm could be heard that solemn familiar voice from Marianne's childhood. It was still shrill and strident with conviction as it spoke of war-winning secret weapons that would turn the tide even at this late hour. It was one of the last broadcasts from the Führer bunker.

We are going to show our enemies that our courage and our spirit are made of Krupp steel. Keep up your morale, Berliners! I am with you!

The official Nazi newspaper, the *Völkischer Beobachter*, echoed its belligerent message that week in large lurid headlines;

'Blood Orgies in the East', 'Soviet Bestialities', 'Gruesome Scenes in a Convent' and 'Eisenhower's Hordes Terrorize German Population'.

The same edition carried features ranging from 'How to Use a Panzerfaust' to 'How to Rejuvenate Your Skin in Spring' and a 'Recipe for Biscuits Without Fat and Eggs'. It was a surreal situation made all the more bizarre by seeing homes and familiar landmarks erased from the landscape overnight. Friends, family and neighbours would be sharing in their misfortune one day and be dead the next. Going out became perilous and girls like Marianne risked their lives in the crossfire for a loaf of bread, though no one was baking fresh bread in the war zone. As Marianne admitted: 'A primordial need for food had inhibited any rational thinking by belittling, if not totally ignoring, the risks involved.'

Within weeks Hitler would be dead and that familiar voice would fade into oblivion. It was remarkable how quickly the German people would forget it when there were more pressing matters to attend to and a life to resume.

CHAPTER TWELVE

Making a Stand

Whether they liked it or not, everyone's existence changed when the Nazis came to power. But it was how people responded to the creeping evil that permeated every facet of German life that made them different.

Author Irmgard Keun rejected the new regimewholeheartedly. She wrote about the horrors of life under the Nazis through the medium of the novel, portraying the day-to-day reality of Hitler's criminal administration while it was still in power.

Melita Maschmann, on the other hand, joined the BDM and became a fanatical Nazi, subscribing totally to the National Socialist lie. Her nationalist fervour even led her to falsely denounce her friend and her friend's family. She too wrote about her experiences under the Nazis, but only after she had driven Polish farmers from their land and served as a propagandist. Her memoir was intended as the apology of a repentant Nazi, but not everyone could forgive her.

The woman who wasn't there

Irmgard Keun was not only a remarkable writer but she was also a remarkable woman. When her best-selling books were banned by the Nazis, she sued the Gestapo for lost royalties, knowing that she had no chance of winning her case. But she felt strongly that someone had to make a public stand against the regime who were burning books in the public squares where once they had burned heretics and witches. She believed in Heinrich Heine's prophetic admonition which stated that: 'Where they burn books they will also ultimately burn people.'

But she did more than protest. In May 1940, she persuaded a British newspaper to publish a fake obituary stating that she had committed suicide in despair following the fall of France. She then obtained a new passport using only her middle and married name, Charlotte Tralow, so that she could return to Germany and live with her parents in Cologne under a false identify, an offence punishable by death. There she lived secretly among her persecutors so that she could write about life under a dictatorship from the inside.

At the age of 26, Keun had seemed destined for a dazzling career. Her debut novel *Gilgi* and its successor, *The Artificial Silk Girl*, were the talk of the literary world. Her shallow, sexually permissive heroines with their pragmatic attitude and loose morals presented a challenge to the traditionalists and seemed to capture the zeitgeist of Germany under the Weimar Republic in the early 1930s. But within two years, Germany was under the heel of a repressive regime and any art that subverted convention or satirized conservative values was condemned as 'anti-German' and 'degenerate' and its creators were made to fear for their lives. The Nazis took particular exception to her thinly veiled attacks on their hypocritical attitude towards women, as in *The Artificial Silk Girl*:

> If a young woman from money married an old man because of money and nothing else and makes love to him for hours and has this pious look on her face, she's called a German mother and a decent woman. If a young woman without money sleeps with a man with no money because he has smooth skin and she likes him, she's a whore and a bitch.

After losing her lawsuit against the Gestapo, she divorced her pro-Nazi husband and emigrated first to Europe and then the United States, where she found a sympathetic audience among the intelligentsia, including fellow exiles Heinrich Mann and Stefan Zweig.

It was while in exile that she wrote her classic account of life under the Nazis, *After Midnight* (1937), a sharp satirical critique of fascist 'philosophy'. Although there are many fine novels set in the Hitler years, few were written during the period and fewer still focused on female characters.

Her heroine, Sanna Moder, is a frivolous 19-year-old girl caught up in the nightmarish years of Hitler's rise to power, when survival meant being seen and heard to advocate Party policy. Through her innocent, uncomprehending eyes the reader glimpses the heady confusion and panic of the days and weeks following Hitler's succession to the Chancellorship, when law and order was transferred to the Gestapo. Over the course of two days the characters' lives are contaminated by the pervasive and poisonous Nazi doctrines.

Sanna's perceptive observations are contrasted with those of two credulous English newspapermen who arrive in Germany to report on the political situation, blithely unaware of the gravity and frightening absurdity of the situation.

As Sanna says at one point: 'I still don't know what it is all about, or what they mean. And it's far too dangerous to ask anyone.'

Sanna may be ingenuous and unworldly, but Keun's masterstroke was to imply that she is not as credulous as the masses who followed Hitler. Through Sanna and her circle of friends Kuhn expressed her own fear for a bleak future instigated by Hitler and his ilk.

GERMAN YOUTH WAS INDOCTRINATED DURING THE HITLER YEARS. MELITA HAD BEEN AN ENTHUSIASTIC MEMBER OF THE BDM SINCE 1933

One dreadful day, revenge will come, and it won't be divine revenge, it will be even more atrocious, more human, more inhuman. And that atrocious revenge which I both desire and fear will necessarily be followed by another atrocious revenge, because the thing that has begun in Germany looks like going on without any hope of an end.

Melita Maschmann – the Nazi who said 'sorry'

It took courage to resist the pressure to conform to the cult of National Socialism and an even greater effort of willpower to reject the incessant and pernicious propaganda with which German youth was indoctrinated during the Hitler years. Incredibly, Melita Maschmann had been an active and enthusiastic member of the BDM since March 1933. Enrolling had been primarily an act of teenage rebellion, to spite her wealthy conservative parents who were members of the German National Party and disapproved of their 15-year-old daughter's desire to enlist in the girl's section of the Hitler Youth. Girls, they told her, had no business joining a military-style group, marching like men and pledging allegiance to a rabble-rousing extremist. Every day her mother would read of yet another political murder in the Berlin morning newspaper and her father would complain of the chaotic scenes in the Reichstag. Their stubborn refusal only intensified Melita's wilful determination to join.

The family seamstress had recruited her.

'For as long as I had known her, she had worn an embossed metal swastika under the lapel of her coat,' Melita would later write. 'That day she wore it openly for the first time and her dark eyes shone as she talked of Hitler's victory.'

But Melita's mother had forbidden her daughter to listen to any more talk of Hitler's 'national community', on the grounds that the 'uneducated' working class and servants in particular had no right to express or hold political views.

BDM membership

Despite their distaste for the Nazis, Melita's parents took their daughter and her twin brother on 30 January to watch thousands of SA troops and Hitler Youth marching through the centre of the city in a torchlight parade to celebrate Hitler's succession to the Chancellorship. She was swept up in its 'sombre pomp' and longed to hurl herself into the current, 'to be submerged and borne along by it', at the same time experiencing 'an intoxicating joy' and a 'burning desire to belong'. In later life, she attempted to find a reason for her devotion and concluded: 'I wanted to escape from my childish, narrow life and I wanted to attach myself to something that was great and fundamental.'

Her nationalism was kindled by a fanciful and sentimental view of her Fatherland as a country 'mysteriously overshadowed with grief, something infinitely dear and threatened with danger'. Melita understood that her generation had been 'fatally prepared to fall victim to [Hitler's] ideas' and that even a girl whose parents had made her politically aware could not hope to resist the lure of fascism.

Melita kept her BDM membership a secret from her family at first, although she considered her commitment to the movement to be an honourable and admirable thing.

> I believed the National Socialists when they promised
> to do away with unemployment ... I believed them
> when they said they would reunite the German nation,
> which had split into more than forty political parties,
> and overcome the consequences of the dictated peace
> of Versailles.

There were an estimated four million unemployed the
year Hitler became Chancellor, a figure equivalent to
the total population of Berlin, and Melita considered her
parent's wilful disregard for their plight to be contemptible.
But her misguided idealism was sorely tested when she
discovered that the National Socialists had no intention
of honouring the socialist policies they had promised to
implement. It was a 'bitter disappointment, the extent of
which I dared not admit to myself'. The evening meetings
held in dank, dark cellars were 'fatally lacking in interest',
and consisted of learning the words to songs ('the linguistic
poverty of which I was unable to ignore'), compiling lists,
dealing with subscriptions and engaging in aimless
political discussions which invariably ended in an
embarrassed silence.

On one occasion, they spent interminable hours
discussing the 'lunatic thesis' that the writer and poet
Goethe had murdered his friend, the dramatist, historian
and philosopher Friedrich Schiller in 1805. Melita
attempted to contest this theory by citing correspondence
between the two men but was laughed down by 'the Old
Guard'. This 'shameless lie' marked the beginning of
Melita's disillusionment with the leadership, if not the
movement itself.

Frustration with fellow members
It seemed that the organization was to provide spectacle but
little substance. Its youthful supporters were there to perform
'tedious duties', to practise drilling like toy soldiers, to make

an appearance at the annual Party rally and to rattle collection tins and pester the public for contributions to the cause, which were often pocketed by Party officials. Their reward for their misguided loyalty and enthusiasm was occasional outings into the countryside, where organized activities included 'hikes, sports, campfires and youth hostelling'. So-called 'Field exercises' often 'degenerated into a first-class brawl', with girls fighting over the flag or some other symbolic prize.

Melita despaired of achieving her ambition to find companionship and like-minded, politically aware people with whom she could discuss and debate her *Welt besser* (better world) views as soon as she discovered that she was the only girl in her section with a secondary school education. The rest were lower middle class young working women with no 'militant class consciousness'.

In her frustration, Melita formed an unofficial discussion group of girls with intellectual pretensions – 'a community of equals' culled from neighbouring groups – but when their existence was discovered Melita was lectured on her disloyalty by the sub-regional leader and transferred to the press division. There she was responsible for supplying news of the organization's activities to regional daily newspapers.

Indoctrination

Although she considered her new role a form of promotion when she might have been dismissed outright, she soon found her co-workers were 'painfully coarse and primitive'. They in turn looked down condescendingly on her because she had joined the movement in March 1933, in the euphoria following the Nazi seizure of power in rigged elections six days after they had staged the Reichstag fire. They had been loyalists from the earlier days of 'the struggle' and resented the so-called 'March violets'. The leaders 'had no marked intellectual interests', Melita observed, 'a fact which natu-rally distressed me in my superiors'.

And yet she 'knuckled under willingly to every authority' while rejecting the influence of the Church, to which she had once been loyal. Such was the efficacy of Nazi indoctrination, which began by appealing to its members' love of Germany but which then soon promoted a hatred for its enemies, both real and imagined. However, she admired some of her superiors, who did not preach hatred or brutality but endured poverty and privation in their poorly-paid positions for a party they believed in. This, she felt, was the 'tragedy' of the Hitler years, that 'so many good people fell victim to the fascination of the Third Reich'.

Melita confessed to having found a meaning and a purpose to her life after a failed love affair and that meaning was inextricably tied to National Socialism. It was no longer necessary for an individual to be happy, she wrote, only to be useful to the state. Her school work suffered as she devoted more time and energy to the BDM, working from 5 a.m. and arriving at school late in the morning, or leaving school early to fulfil her duties.

Her closest friend, Marianne Schweitzer, was appalled when she heard Melita had joined the BDM, not only because the pair had spent hours discussing their adolescent daydreams about how they would make the world a better place but also because Marianne was Jewish and Hitler had declared his intention to remove all Jews from German public life. Marianne could not understand why her friend had betrayed their shared ideals and could not forgive her, even much later, as she told Helen Epstein of the *New Yorker* in May 2013:

I was horrified. She persuaded me to attend meetings where Hitler would speak; her intent was to have me convert. I told her in no uncertain terms that he sounded like a hysterical fanatic and that I couldn't understand how an educated, highly intelligent person like her could possibly be impressed by him. She told me that I was not able to appreciate his greatness because I had Jewish blood.

Turns informer

Marianne hadn't considered herself Jewish and only learned of her heritage after her sister had pleaded with their mother to be allowed to join the BDM. Marianne's family were members of a Lutheran community who regularly attended church and celebrated Easter and Christmas but her paternal grandparents had been Jews. That made their granddaughters *Mischlinge*, or half-Jews, according to Nazi race laws. They were permitted to remain in school, but the family were continually harassed by the Brownshirts after Melita informed the Gestapo that the Schweitzers were holding illegal meetings in their home for anti-Nazi sympathizers.

It was a malicious lie, but it gave the Nazi thugs an excuse to persecute the family at every opportunity. Marianne's father was badly beaten and her mother and older sister were arrested and thrown into a concentration camp. Her mother was released shortly afterwards while her sister remained imprisoned for a year, but it was clearly only a matter of time before they were all rounded up and transported to Auschwitz, so that Propaganda Minister Joseph Goebbels could boast that Berlin was *Judenfrei* (free of Jews).

> **HER GRANDPARENTS HAD BEEN JEWS. THEY WERE PERMITTED TO REMAIN IN SCHOOL, BUT THE FAMILY WERE CONTINUALLY HARASSED BY THE BROWNSHIRTS**

Despite Marianne's best efforts, her sister and one of her brothers chose to remain in Germany. He would die fighting on the Russian front. Her sister survived the war as did her mother and her other brother, who managed to flee the country. Marianne and her father sailed to

England shortly before the outbreak of war in 1939 and then she travelled on alone to America, where she made a new life for herself, never imagining that she would ever hear from her former friend again.

Apologetic memoir

Melita had been removed from her state school in 1936 and sent away to a boarding school, in a last desperate effort by her parents to isolate her from her Nazi associates. But she had been fanatically committed to the cause, in her friend's estimation, and it was therefore a considerable shock for Marianne to receive a letter from her in October 1948 expressing her remorse for having informed on the family and asking if she could renew their friendship. Marianne chose not to reply, nor did she respond to Melita's subsequent letters.

It was not until the spring of 1963, when Marianne returned to Germany in her capacity as a teacher, at the invitation of the Goethe Institute, that they met again. Marianne was sceptical about her friend's show of remorse, remembering that she had learned the black art of propaganda while in the employ of her Nazi masters, and so only very reluctantly read her memoir, *Fazit: Kein Rechtfertigungsversuch* (Account Rendered: A Dossier on my Former Self), prior to its publication.

The book was an extended monologue in the form of an imaginary letter to her former friend, to whom Melita attempted to explain her misguided loyalty.

Even the element of fate in a person's life does not dispose of individual guilt, I know that. What I hope, dare to hope, is that you might be able to understand – not excuse – the wrong and even evil steps which I took and which I must report, and that such an understanding might form the basis for a lasting dialogue.

Melita had much to be ashamed of. During the war, she had been sent to Poland to supervise the forced eviction of farmers and the resettlement of their land by ethnic Germans. She had been in charge of the Women's Labour Service camps between 1941 and 1943 before being reassigned to the BDM's press and propaganda division for the last 18 months of the war. For her part in forging false documents for Nazi fugitives in the immediate post-war period she had been arrested in 1945 and subjected to an intensive denazification course.

But Melita's words did not have the desired effect on Marianne.

> I was utterly shocked by what I read. I hadn't realized the extent of her activities during the war. I was confused, hurt, overwhelmed, and unable to talk about it. She cried when we said goodbye. I did not.

The two women never saw each other again.

> I give her credit for having the courage to write and publish *Fazit* at the time she did. In 1963, nobody I met admitted to having been a Nazi. She may have been the first German, and certainly the first German woman, who tried to face her past with honesty. No other book at that time said, unequivocally, 'I was a Nazi, and here's why.' I am certainly treated well in her memoir, with insight and respect. Melita eventually came to be horrified by Nazism, and I believe she really meant the book as an apology.

Finds peace

In Germany, Melita's memoir was received by some with a mixture of cautious appreciation for its candour, with scepticism by those who saw it as a cynical attempt at self-justification and with bitter resentment by those unrepentant believers who viewed it as a betrayal. It quickly became a bestseller, being reprinted no less than seven times, and was added to the required reading list in many state schools. In America, the eminent Jewish activist and editor Arthur Samuelson acclaimed it as having been written by

> someone who had been overtaken by history. Someone who was struggling to make sense of what no longer made sense, and to understand why it had once done so. And someone whose best self had been attracted to Nazism.

He concluded:

> The memoir seemed believable and honest in ways that other testimonies from the defeated did not.

Melita also established a short correspondence with political philosopher Hannah Arendt, who had formulated her theory of the 'banality of evil' after reporting on the Eichmann war crimes trial two years earlier. The purpose of the book, she told Arendt, was to explain the Nazi mentality and its attraction to those who sought to understand it and also to encourage former Nazis to examine their own motivations. Arendt was convinced that its author was genuine.

'I have the impression that you are totally sincere,' she replied, 'otherwise I would not have written back to you.'

Shortly after its publication, Melita left Germany for India and there became enthralled by a female guru, Sri Anandamayi Ma, at whose behest she took an Indian name and spurned her former life. She, at least, appeared to have come to terms with her Nazi past and found peace.

CHAPTER THIRTEEN

Doves and Eagles - the BDM

In the years before BDM membership became compulsory, many German girls, and their parents too, saw it as some sort of Girl Guides movement, in which adolescent girls could fulfil themselves through pursuits such as hiking, mountaineering and singing around a campfire. But they were soon disillusioned. The true purpose of the organization was to indoctrinate its members with National Socialist ideology, to the detriment of a normal education. Conformity and control pervaded every area of the girls' lives.

Once they reached the age of 18, they had to report to the Reich Labour Service for six months' compulsory employment, where their duties could be unpleasant and even dangerous. Yet others were forced to take part in the Lebensborn SS breeding programme and some even had to fight for the Fatherland.

The enduring image of the *Bund Deutscher Mädel* (League of German Maidens) is that of physically robust young girls with peaches and cream complexions cheerfully participating in various sports and other healthy outdoor activities in their starched and spotless Hitler Youth uniforms. The BDM's motto, 'Be faithful, be pure, be German', does nothing to dispel that notion. Yet the truth was very different.

Not every member of the BDM was seduced by the prospect of singing songs around a campfire, marching to the beat of the Führer's drum or resigning themselves to a life selflessly devoted to *Kinder, Küche, Kirche* (Children, Kitchen, Church). As soon as Germany went to war, the camp fire singalongs and organized sports events ended. By winter 1943, the survivors were likely to be cradling a Panzerfaust anti-tank bazooka and lying face down in the rubble waiting to sacrifice themselves in a futile and pathetic gesture for a leader who had often privately expressed his contempt for his own people.

On 18 March 1945, six weeks before he committed suicide rather than face the reality of defeat for which he was largely responsible, Adolf Hitler railed against the nation he believed had betrayed him.

> If the war is lost, the people will be lost also. It is not necessary to worry about what the people will need for elemental survival. On the contrary, it is better for us to destroy even these things. For this nation has proven itself to be the weaker.

If they could not bring themselves to believe that their beloved Führer had abandoned them and blamed them for the destruction raining down around them, they only had to peer out from their shell holes to see the bodies strung up on the trees and lamp posts, with placards round their necks carrying the words: 'I am too cowardly to defend the capital of the Reich.'

Berlin housewife Dorothea von Schwanenflügel witnessed many summary executions.

> ... boys who were found hiding were hanged as traitors by the SS as a warning that, 'he who was not brave enough to fight had to die'. When trees were not available, people were strung up from lamp posts. They were hanging everywhere, military and civilian, men and women, ordinary citizens who had been executed by a small group of fanatics. It appeared that the Nazis did not want the people to survive because a lost war, by their rationale, was obviously the fault of all of us. We had not sacrificed enough and therefore we had forfeited our right to live, as only the government was without guilt. The *Volkssturm* was called up again, and this time, all boys aged 13 and up had to report as our army was reduced now to little more than children filling the ranks as soldiers.

It wasn't just the boys. The girls of the BDM were expected to do their duty too. It was Hitler's psychosis made manifest – his tragic staging of Wagner's mythical *Götterdämmerung*, which ends with the gods being consumed by flames – and it made no distinction between men of fighting age and children, or between young boys and girls.

Unprecedented popularity

Fifteen years before Hitler's suicide, in 1930, the BDM had been founded as a voluntary youth organization (membership only became compulsory in 1936) with the Führer as its charismatic figurehead, an idealized father figure who provided his 'children' with a sense of purpose and identity. There were two age groups: the main BDM, for girls aged 14–18, and the Jungmädelbund, for girls aged 10–14.

(It is worth noting that Italy too had a fascist youth

organization, the Opera Nazionale Balilla, although it was not a military-styled organization and it did not indoctrinate Italian youth with Mussolini's perverse political ideology. In contrast, Nazi indoctrination began early with the Jungvolk, for children aged 6–10. Nazism was all-encompassing.)

BOYS WHO WERE FOUND HIDING WERE HANGED AS TRAITORS BY THE SS AS A WARNING THAT HE WHO WAS NOT BRAVE ENOUGH TO FIGHT HAD TO DIE

One reason for the unprecedented popularity of the BDM was that it fulfilled a basic need for girls in early adolescence. This generation did not have their own culture for they were neither children nor adults. The Hitler cult offered them an organization to which they could direct their excess energy and idealism with a quasi-religious devotion. Most parents approved, having been sold the idea that it would do their children some good. The BDM would encourage participation in organized sports and foster a sense of community, while giving its members a sense of pride in belonging to a popular movement which was to play a prominent, if decorative, role in celebrating the regeneration of the nation.

The girls were attracted by the uniform and the promise of participating in organized outdoor activities such as hiking, climbing, orienteering and practising survival skills, which had previously been enjoyed only by boys. For some, the prospect of getting out of the city or eating a decent meal was sufficient incentive to join. For others, it was the chance to escape a crowded home, endless chores or an oppressive father who treated his wife and daughters like servants. Few parents objected to the idea that the Gruppenführerinnen (group leaders) might impose military-style discipline on their young members, as they thought it might curb rebelliousness and disobedience in their teenage daughters.

Not all parents were in favour of the BDM, however, but they had little say in the matter if their daughters wanted to join. If they objected too strongly it could be taken as a sign that they opposed the regime and the consequences of that could be dire.

Brainwashing

But the Nazis had not created the Hitler Youth for the benefit of its members. They intended that the state should supplant the traditional family unit and the Church. Both exercised a strong influence and a totalitarian regime could not allow its citizens to challenge its authority, so the state lured the children away from their parents and the Church, which had traditionally provided youth clubs and activities. They were conditioned to look upon the Party and its leader, Adolf Hitler, as their new family and National Socialism as their new religion.

It was not a subtle form of brainwashing, but it was a highly effective one. They were persuaded that their parents no longer had any influence over them, that the older generation held outmoded, even subversive, views and that the outside world was their enemy. Only the Party and its representatives were to be obeyed. They were being manipulated, but few of them were aware of it.

Kirsten Eckermann said that the regime created 'mutual fear and misunderstanding' between parents and children.

> My parents were not stupid, they understood what was going on and they lived with it as best as they could. I know that after several years there were times when perhaps both they and I wished that Hitler was dead.

Unlike the non-political youth organizations in other countries, the BDM discouraged initiative and new ideas.

It was effectively a cult whose purpose was to disseminate the irrational 'philosophy' of one man, whose manifesto was to be thrust down their throats and regurgitated word for word; it could be discussed but never questioned. More damaging was the insistence that education must be confined to National Socialist approved subjects, the Party's revisionist reimagining of history and the spurious sciences. As a result, an entire generation of German women graduated from the state school system as semi-literate, qualified for little more than clerical tasks, factory work and serving behind the counter in a shop or cafe. The weekday evening meetings also prevented girls from completing their homework – though the teachers generally didn't force the issue as they knew the BDM took priority – and the stories that were read to them in those meetings were intended to romanticize self-sacrifice rather than self-fulfilment.

Abuse

Helga Stroh remembered one such story over fifty years later. It was about a German soldier who drowned in a swamp while stifling his cries for help, because he knew the enemy would hear and kill his comrades. It was all for the greater good they were told. The individual didn't count. No sacrifice was too great, for one day 'Germany would inherit the world'.

If the girls expected to find some degree of freedom in the organization, they were soon cruelly disillusioned. Conformity and control were the guiding principles and the rules were strict. No make-up or nail polish was permitted (the Führer frowned upon cosmetics), no jewellery was to be worn, hair length was regulated and any fraternizing with boys was *verboten*.

In *Hitler's Girls*, author Tim Heath suggests that this unnatural restriction and presumably the threat of punishment for disobeying may have 'affected the girls' sexual attitudes in later adolescence'. Their ignorance of sexual matters was compounded by the conspicuous absence of sex education in the national curriculum. Pubescent girls were expected to find out all they needed to know from Nazi biology textbooks, which only described the principles of plant reproduction.

Inevitably, some were abused by their leaders, both male and female, but they remained silent because at the time, in that climate of hysteria and unquestioning obedience to authority, no one would have believed the accuser. Heath writes that:

> There are those who will testify that there probably existed as big a paedophile ring within both ranks [the SA and the Hitler Youth] as would not be out of place in our modern society.

Lesbianism, too, proliferated and became 'a natural resulting regression among some of the girls'. But none of this was common knowledge and so was not a deterrent to those eager to join.

Intimate examinations

Membership was, of course, restricted to girls of 'pure Aryan origin', who were obliged to provide documentary proof of their unsullied ancestry dating back two generations. Birth certificates and other records were required for all branches of the family, to ensure there were no relatives of mixed race or Jewish extraction. Once the paperwork had been thoroughly scrutinized, the girls themselves were submitted to a detailed medical inspection during which their hair, eyes and teeth were studied, detailed measurements were taken and any birthmarks or other distinguishing features were noted.

It was all impersonal and dehumanizing. Some girls as young as ten were subjected to a prolonged and unnecessary examination of their breasts and an intrusive and painful inspection of their genitals by male doctors, although there was no medical justification for this. Anita von Schoener was given an examination of this nature by an SS doctor who told her that she was 'a special child' who would be sure to 'have lots of German children' for the Führer. But she regarded it as 'totally absurd' for the doctor to have needed to confirm that she had not lost her virginity at that age. When she realized that she had been chosen for the Lebensborn SS breeding programme she resented being one of those girls who had been selected to produce offspring 'whether we liked it or not'. According to Tim Heath, some of those who were encouraged to produce as many illegitimate children as possible were as young as 14 and many were no older than 19.

Anita admitted that she 'had no answers' to her questions concerning her former Jewish friends, whom she was forbidden to talk to. She was aware too that she did not have the maturity or knowledge to challenge what she was being taught, 'yet I understood perfectly the differences between right and wrong'. And so too did her teachers and those Nazi leaders who visited the school and BDM meetings to lecture the girls on the new morality, such as Hitler Youth leader Baldur von Schirach, Heinrich Himmler and Dr Goebbels. Unable to justify their persecution of the outsiders, they merely appealed to the girls' sense of duty and reminded them of their oath of unquestioning obedience. They were 'adjusting our moral sense', as Anita saw it. And for those who were not so easily convinced, they were reminded of the fate of Sophie Scholl who 'betrayed' her BDM comrades and her Fatherland by spreading seditious 'lies'. Scholl, they were told, was not a Jew but a German citizen.

(Sophie Scholl became a BDM member when she was at school, like most of her classmates, but soon became disillusioned with the Nazi Party. She became concerned about the Nazis' treatment of her Jewish friends and other

Jews and the fact that an evil regime was enslaving and destroying Germany. These feelings were intensified when her father was arrested for criticizing Hitler. She was also horrified by first-hand reports of German war crimes on the Eastern Front. While she was a student she became involved with the White Rose, an informal group that had been founded by her brother, Hans Scholl, and others. Its aims were to oppose the war and the Nazi regime. The group members wrote six anti-Nazi leaflets and distributed them across Munich. On 18 February 1943 Sophie and other members of the group were arrested and tried. Early the following morning they were executed by guillotine.)

Having satisfied the stringent requirements, the successful candidate would be inducted during a simple ceremony at which she would swear a personal oath of allegiance to Hitler, thereby aligning her fate with that of her Führer. In this way, Hitler was able to exploit their loyalty to the extent that some of them sacrificed their lives in that final and futile last stand in spring 1945.

Precision routines

Much importance was placed on synchronized gymnastic routines requiring strength, balance and precision to create visually impressive formations. As with everything in Hitler's Reich it was all about appearances. The girls were also taught drilling and how to march in unison, but for whose benefit were these precision routines performed? By all accounts, the girls didn't particularly enjoy taking part or benefit in any way. It was hard, demanding work and it took hours to perfect the displays which were performed mainly for the press and Party officials. The BDM was a purely ornamental organization and served what one young BDM member described as 'the Nazis' obsession with young females'.

If the girls had imagined that they would be admired by their male counterparts in the Hitler Youth, they were often sadly disappointed. Many found themselves the object of crude sexual banter and taunts, which revealed how little the boys thought of their female comrades. The BDM soon became an acronym for rude alternatives; *Bedarfsartikel Deutscher Männer* (requisite for German males), *Bald Deutsche Mutter* (German mothers to be) and such like.

Every activity in the BDM summer camps was strictly regimented with fines and extra duties imposed for infractions of discipline and tardiness. The camps were supplemented by specially-built schools, where the curriculum was confined to political ideology, domestic science and childcare. Girls with no experience of caring for a younger sibling were billeted with families who had several children.

Compulsory employment

Once the older girls had reached the age of 18 they were required to report for work with the RAD (Reich Labour Service) for six months' compulsory 'employment', for which they were paid a nominal wage. By 1940, there were nine million girls working on the land or in the armaments industry. Within a few years many of those in agricultural placements would be forcibly reassigned to farms in the occupied countries to the East where they witnessed – or even participated in – forced evictions, transportations and atrocities committed by both the Wehrmacht and the SS.

> ONE AFTERNOON INGEBORG WATCHED AS ONE OF THE SS DOGS BEGAN PAWING AT THE GROUND. WITHIN MINUTES IT HAD UNEARTHED HUMAN REMAINS

Ingeborg Schaller was 19 years old when she was sent to an unidentified destination in the East, where she and a number of other girls were told to clean the homes of the previous inhabitants in readiness for their new occupants. One afternoon, she watched as one of the SS dogs began pawing at the ground. Within moments it had unearthed human remains that had clearly been hastily buried. Whether it was the body of a man, a woman or a child, she did not know. However, after the war the site was excavated and 'a large number' of bodies were discovered there, all of them people who had been murdered by the SS. Neighbouring sites were also investigated, revealing a similar story. Ingeborg told her parents when she returned home and was warned not to discuss it with anyone.

Farm work was no easy option. It was just as gruelling as factory work, but it had its advantages. There was little risk of air raids and the food could be exceptionally good, if you were lucky. Many girls ate turkey, rabbit, duck and goose for the first time in their lives during those years and when their assignment came to an end some chose to remain on the farms rather than return to the towns and cities where they would be required to report for the munitions assembly lines.

The girls who were chosen for this work found that their smaller hands were put to use polishing the inside of shells. But even after the safety procedures had been explained to them, there were horrific accidents. Their tasks were often tedious, and the noise and smell could be extremely unpleasant, leading to chronic headaches and fatigue. They felt ill-treated until they saw the slave labourers, who worked far longer hours, were given little food or water and were forced to work through air raids while the paid workers ran for the shelters.

Other girls in the RAD fared better, particularly when they were assigned to driving buses and trams, but they were often prey to the unwanted attentions of lecherous males who had only one thing on their minds.

CHAPTER FOURTEEN

Swelling the Ranks

In order to stem the falling birth rate and replenish the ranks of the Wehrmacht, Himmler came up with the idea of the Lebensborn programme. German girls of child-bearing age were encouraged to have intercourse with selected partners, often SS officers. In the end the enterprise proved a failure, as limited numbers of children were born under the scheme and for some reason many of those were of low intelligence. After the war, the children were ostracized because they were a reminder of a Nazi past.

Hildegard Trutz – giving birth for Hitler

On leaving school in the summer of 1936, 18-year-old Hildegard Trutz was offered what must qualify as the most bizarre careers advice in history. On admitting that she did not know what job to take, her local BDM leader suggested that she 'give the Führer a child'. What the Reich needed, she was told, was 'racially sound stock'. Hildegard admitted that she was 'mad about Adolf Hitler and the new better Germany', and so was willing to serve him in any way she could – even if it meant sleeping with strangers and enduring the pain of giving birth only to have the child taken away for adoption by state-sanctioned foster parents.

She was an ardent convert to National Socialism and a more than willing advocate of their rabid racist ideology. As she later told childhood friend Louis Hagen:

> As time went on more and more girls joined the BDM, which gave us a great advantage at school. The mistresses were mostly pretty old and stuffy. They wanted us to do scripture and, of course, we refused. Our leaders had told us that no one could be forced to listen to a lot of immoral stories about Jews, and so we made a row and behaved so badly during scripture classes that the teacher was glad in the end to let us out. Of course, this meant another big row with Mother ... But the real row with Mother came when the BDM girls refused to sit on the same bench as the Jewish girls at school ... We knew we were right to have nothing to do with either of them. In the end, we got what we wanted. We began by chalking 'Jews out!' or 'Jews perish, Germany awake!' on the blackboard before class ... In the end three other girls and I went to the Headmaster and told him that our Leader would report the matter to the Party authorities unless he removed this stain from the school. The next day the two girls stayed away, which made me very proud of what we had done.

Hildegard was at the forefront of her local unit and enjoying a prominent role in its activities. Her height and Nordic features brought her to the attention of the national BDM magazine, *Das Deutsche Mädel*, which featured her photograph in one issue and intensified her devotion to the organization and to National Socialism.

'When we had any street collections my box was always full first and I worked on the other girls to buck up so that our group always made a good impression wherever we went.'

These collections were organized on an almost weekly basis and donations were pursued with excessive zeal. Whoever refused to contribute was considered to be a Communist or a Jew and was intimidated and beaten up by SA thugs.

Ideal breeding stock

Becoming a surrogate mother for the Fatherland appealed to the Berlin schoolgirl, who was considered 'ideal Aryan breeding stock' because of her broad child-bearing hips, her racially pure blood and her Nordic features, although she would have to be prepared to submit to medical tests to confirm her racial suitability. All candidates were also required to provide a certificate of Aryan ancestry dating back to their great-grandparents and sign a document attesting to the fact that there was no history of hereditary disease or mental illness in the family. Even so, six out of every ten applicants were rejected.

> **ALL CANDIDATES WERE REQUIRED TO PROVIDE A CERTIFICATE OF ARYAN ANCESTRY DATING BACK TO THEIR GREAT-GRANDPARENTS**

'It sounded wonderful,' she later recalled, though at the time she had not heard of the state-authorized breeding project known as Lebensborn (fountain of life), which was intended to increase the falling birth rate and replenish the ranks in the coming war.

The programme had been the pet project of SS Reichsführer Heinrich Himmler, who took a special interest in Aryan children born on his birthday and a less than healthy interest in his men's choice of partners. His inquisitiveness bordered on the voyeuristic and his approval of their marriages was subject to peculiar preferences and prejudices against women who wore too much make-up and dressed to look like movie queens.

It had been his idea to reverse both the declining birth rate and the dramatic increase in abortions by giving the young, often unwed, mothers the opportunity to give birth in a state-sponsored clinic and have the babies adopted by suitable Aryan foster parents. During the interwar years abortions in Germany had risen to an all-time high of 800,000. From this grew the notion of selective interbreeding to swell the ranks of the SS.

Dismisses mother's objections

Even with Himmler's endorsement many German parents would have had serious misgivings about allowing their daughters to participate in what was little more than state-sponsored prostitution. Hildegard feared that her parents would disapprove and so she decided to keep her involvement a secret and instead told them that she was going away on a residential course to study political ideology.

Hildegard's father worked in a large bakery employing many people and was continually complaining about his low wages and the fact that he could barely feed his family on what he was paid. His daughter in her turn had little expectation of improving their circumstances if she remained at home and looked for a job. Her mother, though, was devoutly religious and distrusted the Nazis, who had voiced their opposition to the Catholic Church and made it known that they intended to replace it with the secular National Socialist credo and Teutonic pagan-like services. This would see the cross discarded for the swastika and the Bible succeeded by *Mein Kampf*. Frau Trutz had objected to her daughter joining the BDM in 1933, arguing that the Party was

> FRAU TRUTZ HAD OBJECTED TO HER DAUGHTER JOINING THE BDM IN 1933, ARGUING THAT THE PARTY WAS ATTEMPTING TO SUPPLANT THE FAMILY

attempting to supplant the family while professing to value tradition and the role of the mother, but her husband had been persuaded by a family friend, a member of the SA, that it was Hildegard's duty to enrol.

Hildegard dismissed her mother's objections, knowing that her father would have the final word.

> We were the new youth; the old people just had to learn to think in the new way and it was our job to make them see the ideals of the new nationalized Germany. When I told her about the camp with the Hitler Youth she was shocked. Well, suppose a young German youth and a German girl did come together and the girl gave a child to the Fatherland – what was so very wrong in that? When I tried to explain that to her she wanted to stop me going on in the BDM – as if it was her business! Duty to the Fatherland was more important to me and, of course, I took no notice.

Luxury accommodation

Other girls in the movement felt the same. Ilse Heimerdinger (later McKee) later wrote:

> We were Germany's hope in the future, and it was our duty to breed and rear the new generation of sons and daughters. These lessons soon bore fruit in the shape of quite a few illegitimate small sons and daughters for the Reich, brought forth by teenage members of the League of German Maidens. The girls felt they had done their duty and seemed remarkably unconcerned about the scandal.

Indeed, 900 girls between the ages of 15 and 18 returned from the 1936 Nuremberg Rally to discover they were pregnant. Those who chose to have their baby in one of the 14 Lebensborn clinics established in Germany and Austria were able to avoid a family scandal and also the responsibility of bringing up the child, which would be adopted by state-sanctioned foster parents.

When Hildegard arrived at the Lebensborn centre in Tegernsee in Bavaria, she learned that she was one of 40 young women staying at an old castle which had been converted into a luxury hostel. Few of the girls had experienced such luxury before and they soon became accustomed to being waited on by servants and offered the finest food some of them had ever tasted. The facilities were equally impressive, with a music room, a gymnasium and a cinema. For working- and middle-class girls who were used to having to help their mothers with the chores it was a thrill to be pampered and indulged like a movie star.

Any reservations they had regarding the forced adoption of their babies were offset by the belief that the infants would be reared in state institutions for the greater good of the Reich.

Choosing a partner

The SS doctors who examined them and supervised the pregnancies believed that conception was more likely to be successful if the girl was relaxed and willing to have intercourse with her chosen mate and so the prospective partners were introduced socially. They were encouraged to get to know one another in the week before they were paired off, although it was forbidden for both parties to reveal their real names. The only thing the girls were told about their partners was that they were SS officers. Some of these men were married.

Hildegard's choice was a tall, physically impressive handsome young man, but someone she decided was not the brightest of the bunch. However, it was not his conversation that appealed to her. Ten days after her period she was given another medical examination before approval was given for them to sleep together.

'As both the father of my child and I believed completely in the importance of what we were doing, we had no shame or inhibitions of any kind.'

To increase the chance of a successful conception they had sex for three successive nights, then he was sent to sleep with another girl.

> **TWO WEEKS AFTER SHE HAD GIVEN BIRTH TO A HEALTHY BOY, HILDEGARD WILLINGLY GAVE HIM TO THE NURSE AND NEVER SAW HIM AGAIN**

Once her pregnancy was confirmed, she left the comfort of the castle and was transferred to a maternity unit where she was monitored for the next nine months. No anaesthetics were offered during labour in case it adversely affected the child, but Hildegard accepted this as part of her sacrifice for the Fatherland. Two weeks after she had given birth to a healthy boy she willingly gave him to the nurse and never saw him again.

Himmler's 'children'

Within months of her return to Berlin she met and married SS officer Ernst Trutz, who apparently did not share her sense of pride or honour in having a wife who had produced a son for Hitler's elite. After the war, those who were identified as such found themselves stigmatized by a nation desperate to forget its Nazi past. More significantly, many of Himmler's 'children' were far short of being prime specimens of the Aryan master race, but were of lower than average intelligence, whether due to genetics or their upbringing. It was the one thing Himmler, the former chicken farmer, had not factored into the equation.

Louis Hagen met Hildegard Trutz again in 1946 and found her physically much changed.

Her straggly bleached hair was screwed up into a knot, her face was sallow and unhealthy looking and her teeth were terrible. She looked the perfect picture of a slut, with her grimy bare feet and filthy ragged dress.

But her National Socialist ardour had not, evidently, cooled.

She did not recognize me at first ... She began by inquiring after my family but as soon as I mentioned that some of them had been gassed by the Nazis, she changed the subject at once and began to talk about her own troubles.

Brown Sisters

The Nazis placed great significance on the role of mothers in their New Order. They rewarded the most fecund with medals and they enticed young girls (the majority of whom were unmarried) to mate with virile members of the SS, in order to produce blond, blue-eyed Aryan males to fill their ranks. But the enterprise proved a failure with only 8,000 babies born in the German maternity homes and 10,000 in Sweden. The yield produced by additional 'breeding clinics' in Norway, Belgium, Holland, Luxembourg, Denmark and France is unknown. Altogether, a rather poor result for such a large investment.

Unwilling to wait to see if the experiment was a success, Reichsführer Himmler ordered the abduction of suitable children from the conquered countries in eastern Europe. They would be adopted by approved Aryan couples who would raise them as their own and never reveal their true identity, origin or parentage. Some 200,000 children with characteristic Nordic features were stolen from Poland alone.

This process of 'Germanization' was entrusted to the female members of the NSV, the National Socialist People's

Welfare organization, who would tell the older children that their parents were dead or had abandoned them. The younger ones would grow up believing that their foster parents were their real parents. Those children who failed the stringent racial medical examinations were sent to their deaths in concentration and extermination camps.

In scenes reminiscent of a Grimm fairy tale these Nazi nurses, commonly known as the 'Brown Sisters' because of their brown uniforms, scoured the towns and villages of Poland and Slovenia in the wake of the Wehrmacht and attempted to lure children out of hiding with bread and sweets.

CHAPTER FIFTEEN

Women as Bringers of Death

Ethics is concerned with right and wrong, but establishing what is morally right can be a challenge.

This would not appear to present a problem for the nursing profession, however, where a nurse's duty is to care for patients. Yet the nurses who were involved in the Nazi euthanasia project claimed that they were bound by an entirely different code of ethics. Their duty of care was to the health of the state, which meant that unhealthy or diseased bodies had to be eradicated.

Other women brought death in different ways, for instance as members of the Werwolf units who stayed behind after Germany had fallen to the Allies, carrying out sabotage and assassination missions. Some of them used their youth and beauty to scout out chosen areas or get close to an assassination target.

The shudder house

As well as abducting children, nurses were also active in the Nazi euthanasia project, in which an estimated 300,000 people were murdered in asylums, nursing homes and paediatric wards under the pretext that they were 'unworthy of life'. Very few of their murderers were prosecuted after the war and still fewer were made to account for their crimes or required to explain how they could reconcile their role as carers with their participation in unjustifiable 'mercy killings'.

Irmgard Huber was arguably the most prominent participant to be named in the international press when she was indicted for murder during the Hadamar Trial. The case was the first major war crimes trial to be held in the US zone of Germany, preceding the Nuremberg trials by a year. It took its name from the institution where Huber was employed as head nurse; a former sanatorium where she claimed to have been spared from direct involvement in the terminations by the director's assistant, Alphons Klein, a Gestapo agent with whom she was having an affair.

She was then about 45 years old and was described by one reporter as 'about six foot tall and built like a football player' and 'as ugly as a witch'. In contrast to the callous harpies who worked as concentration camp guards, Huber impressed the court as a woman who appeared to be genuinely contrite. It was said that she gave cakes to the children who were to be killed in an effort to cheer them up and she was tearful all through the trial. At one point, according to the *Los Angeles Times*, she wailed: 'I worked all the time under compulsion ... where could I go?'

When the Americans stumbled upon the facility one Sunday in late March 1945, they found head nurse Huber and the entire staff working as if nothing had changed. As Private George Jaeger, translator for the American

Fifth Corps War Crime Unit observed, the staff were evidently relying on the 'credibility of their insane asylum cover to protect them from being discovered'. But the real purpose of the facility was exposed by a former trustee, a captured French intelligence officer who had feigned insanity to survive in the 'shudder house' where at least 15,000 people had been murdered by lethal injection or gassed in the basement.

The ABC murders

The first phase of the murderous operation had involved the killing of approximately 10,000 mentally and physically handicapped German citizens, whose bodies were burned in the ovens of the crematorium.

The second phase saw the gassing of around 5,000 Eastern European and Russian slave workers who had been deemed unfit for further work in the factories of the Ruhr due to sickness, starvation or exhaustion and were to be disposed of in a similar fashion.

They were brought to Hadamar in trucks under cover of darkness, so as not to arouse the curiosity of the local inhabitants; up to 70 'patients' at a time. On arrival they were assured that they had been brought to the institution for rest and medical treatment and were allocated a bed in a sparsely furnished and unheated ward isolated from the rest of the inmates. Shortly after they were dressed and fed they would be given a lethal injection of Scopolamine, a derivative of belladonna known as 'the Devil's Breath' for its ability to incapacitate the patient. But the crematorium couldn't cope with the amount of corpses and the locals complained about

ON ARRIVAL THEY WERE ASSURED THAT THEY HAD BEEN BROUGHT TO THE INSTITUTION FOR REST AND MEDICAL TREATMENT AND WERE ALLOCATED A BED

the acrid smoke, so the trustees were employed in digging mass graves in which the bodies were stacked.

Fortunately for the War Crimes Unit, the names of all those who had perished at Hadamar had been recorded with clinical efficiency in files stored in two safes, which the staff had not thought necessary to destroy. The cause of death in the majority of cases was listed as TB or pneumonia, but clerk Adolph Merkle had unwittingly given the game away.

In his efforts to disguise so many suspicious deaths in a single day he had carefully recorded small batches at a time and falsified the dates, but he had foolishly selected them in alphabetical order.

Murder trial

Hadamar was one of six similar sites in Germany which together had witnessed the extermination of up to a quarter of a million people, including 722 *Mischling* (mixed blood) children from Vienna, some of whose brains had been preserved for 'racial studies'.

Huber and all the other nurses involved in the killings attempted to justify their actions by assuring themselves that their duty of care was to the state and not to their patients. In 1938 the regime had issued an edict defining nursing practice, the primary diktat being that nurses were to ensure the purity of the Aryan race. The health of the state had to be preserved and unhealthy or diseased bodies had to be humanely eradicated. Their duty was to the institution and their only duty to their patients was to make them comfortable and show them acts of kindness. However, at the subsequent trials it was revealed that many patients had died as the result of deliberate neglect.

The murder of German civilians by their own people was not considered to be prosecutable in international law, but the killing of the Polish and Russian slave workers did come under Allied jurisdiction. Huber, however, was released after her co-workers testified that she had not taken an active role in the killings; but then she was rearrested when it transpired that she had selected the patients to be killed, controlled the drugs and falsified the death certificates. She was prosecuted for conspiracy to murder and sentenced to 25 years in prison while Alphons Klein and two male nurses were sentenced to death by hanging. The chief doctor, Adolf Wahlmann, received a life sentence but due to his advanced age it was subsequently commuted.

Huber received eight additional years from a German court in 1947, in a subsequent trial in which she was accused of assisting in the murder of at least 120 German citizens. She was released in 1957 after having served only five years.

The Brown Sister

Another nurse, Pauline Kneissler, who was believed to have killed severely wounded German soldiers in a hospital on the Russian front, was tried separately, sentenced to three years for her part in the killings at Hadamar and released a year later. At her trial Kneissler's superiors testified to her willingness to obey orders without question, due to what they considered to be her greatest asset – her indifference to the fate of her patients. She was quoted as saying:

> I never saw mercy killing as murder ... Most important in my life was devotion and self-sacrifice ... I was never cruel to people and for that I will suffer and suffer.

Kneissler, a municipal nurse from Berlin who had proudly worn her Party badge since 1937, was also accused of willing participation in the killing of almost 10,000 patients at the Grafeneck Castle asylum near Stuttgart in 1940. Kneissler had volunteered to tour institutions for the mentally disabled and select up to 70 'useless eaters' a day to be transported to Grafeneck and gassed.

Midwives, too, participated in infanticide on a biblical scale, falsely reporting birth defects in newborn babies as well as recommending unnecessary abortions and sterilizations if the mothers were deemed unsuitable to bear racially pure children.

Ilse Hirsch – the female 'werewolf'

With her long blonde braided hair and piercing blue eyes, 22-year-old Ilse Hirsch made a perfect poster girl for the BDM. She had been featured on the front cover of at least one Nazi propaganda magazine, but in the dying weeks of the war she hoped she would not be recognized. She was on a secret mission (tagged Operation Carnival) to liquidate a 'traitor' as a member of an elite assassination squad, one of the so-called 'Werwolf' units; Nazi guerrillas whom SS Reichsführer Heinrich Himmler had entrusted with the defence of the crumbling Reich.

It was a fitting name, for American Intelligence personnel routinely referred to Germany as 'Transylvania', to denote the ever-present danger posed by 'fifth columnists' and former SS men in civilian clothes. Rumours were rife that fanatical Nazis were hiding among the civilian population and waiting for their chance to launch surprise attacks on unsuspecting, inexperienced rookies who had just been shipped in to replace battle-weary veterans.

The US War Department routinely screened information films for the occupying troops. One such film was *Your Job in Germany*, which warned GIs to be ever vigilant and suspicious.

> Every German is a potential source of trouble. The German people are not our friends. ... However

friendly, however 'sorry', however sick of the Nazi Party they may seem, they cannot come back into the civilized fold just by sticking out their hand and saying, 'I'm sorry'. Sorry? Not sorry they caused the war; only sorry they lost it!'

It went on to remind them that just one mistake might cost a soldier his life. It was a timely warning, as many homesick GIs may have been tempted to fraternize with the pretty young Fräuleins who offered home comforts and perhaps more in exchange for nylons and cigarettes.

With her open smile and slim figure, Ilse must have tempted the young American soldiers to question those orders as they watched her walking into the German Dutch–Belgian border town of Aachen on the morning of 21 March 1945. She had divested herself of her Luftwaffe uniform within moments of being dropped by parachute with the rest of her unit and was now in a drab grey skirt and blouse. She had also had the presence of mind to pick up a discarded basket on her way into town and so looked like any young German girl going to the market. The smiles she exchanged with the GIs were not entirely phoney. Aachen was near her home town of Monschau and it pleased her to return to the region and see that it still retained its familiar sites, although many buildings and houses had been reduced to rubble.

> WITH HER OPEN SMILE AND SLIM FIGURE, ILSE MUST HAVE TEMPTED THE YOUNG AMERICAN SOLDIERS TO QUESTION THOSE ORDERS NOT TO FRATERNIZE

She had been assigned to scout out the house of the intended target, Franz Oppenhoff, a former lawyer who had opposed the Nazis in open court before the war and who had only escaped being transported to a concentration camp by abandoning his legal career and volunteering to work in an armaments factory. He had been invited to return to Aachen in October 1944 by the Allies, to take up the post of mayor and supervise reconstruction. Hitler had been incensed to hear of it and had ordered Himmler to have Oppenhoff killed as an example to other potential 'traitors'.

The plan to assassinate him had been entrusted to SS Obergruppenführer Hans-Adolf Prützmann and the team had been assembled and trained in sabotage and survival skills at Hülchrath Castle near Erkelenz. Supplies were accumulated in underground bunkers in the Eifel and the so-called Alpine Redoubt in Bavaria, where the SS were expected to stage a last stand.

Nazi assassination

As Ilse walked up and down outside the new Bürgermeister's house at 251 Eupener Strasse, noting the possible escape routes and assessing the risk of being interrupted by Allied soldiers, she heard the one sound she feared more than any other at that moment.

'*Ilse!*' Someone was calling her by name in the open street. '*Ilse, bist du das?*' ('Ilse is that you?) '*Was machst du hier?*' ('What are you doing here?')

It was a friend and former fellow member of the BDM. Her momentary happiness at meeting her old comrade was offset by the fear of discovery and so she quickly ushered the girl aside. Ilse was offered a place to stay that night, which would enable her to relax and collect herself before the assassination, which had been set for the next morning. Meanwhile, her five male comrades had buried their parachutes and were sleeping in the forest on the outskirts of the town. Shortly after landing in a forest west of Aachen they had killed a young Dutch border guard who had challenged them and his female companion had run off to sound the alarm, but there were so many isolated incidents in the area that the Americans didn't consider it worth sending out a patrol.

SS sergeant Joseph Leitgeb, a 30-year-old veteran of the Russian front, and 16-year-old Hitler Youth member Erich Morgenschweiss were sent into town to scout the area and bring Ilse back to their camp to report and share her assessment of the situation. Their commander was SS-Untersturmführer Herbert Wenzel, the oldest and most experienced member of the team, which also included SS privates Georg Heidorn and Karl-Heinz Henneman, both of whom were familiar with the area and would serve as guides.

But as the time for the assassination drew near Heidorn lost his nerve and Wenzel was forced to leave him behind at the camp with Erich and Ilse.

When darkness fell, Henneman, Leitgeb and Wenzel made their way into town dressed in their Luftwaffe flying suits, intending to pose as a downed bomber crew seeking shelter at the Oppenhoffs' home. After cutting the phone line they broke in through a cellar window, but their intended target was not at home. They found only his three children and the maid, who was sent to fetch the Bürgermeister. He arrived with a neighbour who excused himself, presumably so he could report the arrival of the German airmen to the Americans, while the maid was sent inside to keep an eye on the children. The two gunmen played for time until the neighbour was out of sight by asking Oppenhoff to lead them back to their own lines, but he refused, insisting that the war was lost and urging them to turn themselves over to the Americans.

Wenzel saw his chance and drew his automatic but he lost his nerve and couldn't pull the trigger when face to face with his intended victim. At that moment Leitgeb grabbed the gun from him and shot Oppenhoff through the head at point-blank range.

Trial and sentencing

The team disappeared in the confusion just minutes before an American patrol arrived and after an eventful journey all but Leitgeb returned to their own lines. He was killed after stepping on a landmine. Ilse triggered an anti-personnel device the next day and was gravely injured, so the others had to leave her behind. They were also badly wounded but they just about managed to stagger on. She

> LEITGEB WAS KILLED AFTER STEPPING ON A LANDMINE. ILSE TRIGGERED AN ANTI-PERSONNEL DEVICE THE NEXT DAY AND WAS GRAVELY INJURED

survived, however, thanks to the intervention of a local farmer, who took her back to town where her wounds were treated.

Wenzel was never seen again. He had prudently given each of his comrades a different account of his origins and history so that he would be difficult to trace. The others, however, were eventually identified as the assassins, and in 1949 they were tracked down and indicted for murder.

The trial took place in Aachen, where Morgenschweiss appeared for the prosecution to save his skin. Contrary to expectations the accused only received nominal sentences even though they were found guilty, as their defence counsel was able to provide a witness who testified that their victim had been seen wearing a Wehrmacht uniform shortly before his death, and was therefore guilty of desertion under Nazi laws. Henneman received 18 months and Heidorn a year, while Ilse Hirsch was sentenced to four years' imprisonment and then acquitted.

The killing of Oppenhoff had received world-wide coverage, which was far more than the team could have imagined, and to capitalize on it Nazi propaganda minister Joseph Goebbels had authorized the launch of Radio Werwolf, a transmitter broadcasting misinformation whose call sign was an unnerving howl. Its message was a repeated call to arms aimed at German youth, whom it urged to 'destroy the enemy or destroy yourselves'. But there were no further officially sanctioned assassinations, though the Werwolf units remained a scare story which kept the Allies on their guard long after the surrender was signed on 7 May 1945.

The one and only successful operation carried out by the Werwolf death squads was in retrospect a futile exercise. Unknown to Ilse and her comrades, the Allies had already determined that Oppenhoff was not to be trusted and were intending to replace him.

The mad maid of Monschau

The medieval town of Monschau near the Belgian border bred a particularly rabid species of Nazi worshipper. Ilse Hirsch was not its only fanatical Hitler devotee.

Teenager Maria Bierganz had been added to a list of suspects drawn up by the American Counter Intelligence Corps in January 1945, after she had been seen talking to a Hitler Youth leader who was subsequently arrested for sabotage. When the CIC searched her home they found a diary which appeared to convict the former BDM girl in her own words.

Her journal detailed the meetings of a resistance organization calling itself Klub Heimat Treue (Club Homeland Loyalty), which she had helped found, and identified Monschau residents who had been fraternizing with the occupation forces. But she reserved her most vitriolic outbursts for the 'amis', or Americans, whom she accused of being cowardly in the face of the V1 offensive and blithely oblivious to the hatred that their civilian population harboured towards them. Most alarmingly, she recorded the oath that this subdivision of the Werwolf organization had sworn, which was to fight to the death.

Each entry took the form of unmailed letters to her lover in the SS, referred to only by his Christian name, Peter. But after two months of intense questioning and investigations the Americans concluded that both Peter and the KHT were an adolescent girl's fantasy. They released her on 4 March, still ablaze with National Socialist ardour and emboldened in her defiance by the knowledge that Goebbels himself had named her as a 'martyr' to their lost cause.

In a broadcast to the beleaguered nation in February 1945 the 'poison dwarf', as he was known to his enemies in the regime, had recast the pathetic teen as a modern-day Joan of Arc who had defied her Allied accusers in an imaginary trial in which, burning with a 'righteous anger', she had warned them that a fourth Reich would rise from the ruins. But by this time few were listening and those who were could hear a hollow ring to his words as the approaching air raids and artillery barrages intensified.

CHAPTER SIXTEEN

Child Soldiers

In a last desperate stand against the advancing enemy the Nazi regime threw every available German into the deadly maelstrom of war. Children as young as eight years old were put into uniform and handed a weapon. The threat of summary execution meant that some went unwillingly to their deaths, but there was still no shortage of eager recruits, including many girls.

The American GIs who faced them were reluctant to engage girls and children in combat, but a rifle in a child's hands was no less lethal than if it had been carried by a trained soldier, so in the end they did what was necessary to defend themselves.

But all German sacrifice was in vain, because the final defeat of Hitler's regime was inevitable. Any girls who managed to survive had to face yet another foe – the Soviet hordes whose idea of vengeance was the violation of the fallen nation's womanhood.

'If it has to be, then the enemies of Germany will drown in the blood of German youth.'

(Adolf Hitler, 1945)

Had Germany won the war, the female factory workers, the land girls and the young women driving the buses and trams would presumably have been discharged as soon as the men returned from the front. Those deemed fit for the Lebensborn programme would have been enticed to continue serving the SS in order to replace the countless fatalities, but the majority of BDM and Jungmädelbund members would probably have resumed their duties at the annual Party rally and all other ceremonial occasions such as the Führer's birthday and victory parades.

However, the war did not go the way Hitler had hoped and his once invincible army, formidable navy and glorious Luftwaffe were routed and in retreat by the spring of 1945. In desperation, the regime threw everything they could at the advancing Allies in a futile and bloody defence of the encircled Reich. Young girls were already serving as auxiliaries in the Wehrmacht and the Luftwaffe, with some manning anti-aircraft guns in the defence of German cities. But with the establishment of the 'Werwolf' guerrilla units in February 1945 both boys and girls as young as eight were drafted in. They were given an undersized uniform and armed with whatever weapons had been salvaged from fallen members of the *Volkssturm*, which consisted mainly of old men, for the regime's last stand.

With weapons and ammunition severely depleted, the defenders had to improvise by making Molotov cocktails from empty bottles filled with petrol with a rag for a fuse, setting booby traps primed with grenades or burying bullets which were triggered by stepping on a nail.

Angel snipers

When officers of the old guard protested that untrained and inexperienced girls should not be fighting in the front line, Hitler is said to have told them that they had as much right to die for their Führer as any man. Many of the girls would be trained in weapons and tactics by army personnel while some were instructed by the 'Brown Sisters', the nurses who were active in the Lebensborn programme and in the forced removal of Aryan-looking children from the occupied countries.

If their faint-hearted pupils were tempted to put down their weapons and return to their shattered homes they were dissuaded by the threat of summary execution. A Führer directive said to have been dictated to Hitler Youth leader Artur Axmann (Baldur von Schirach's successor) declared that if Germany's youth failed to defend the Fatherland then they did not deserve to survive. They were to stand and fight or face death for desertion.

But there were plenty of eager recruits and some were more than capable of competing for kills with the men.

Helga Bassler's father had taught her how to hunt wild boar and to shoot more accurately than most soldiers, so she volunteered to devote her skills to the service of her Führer as an *Engel Heckenschütze* (angel sniper). Predictably, her prowess was resented by her male comrades, who made no effort to hide their frustration, especially when she demonstrated her superiority on the firing range and casually informed them that anyone could learn to shoot as well with a little patience and a lot of practice.

Girl tank-busters

Those girls who did not possess such skills, or who discovered that the rifles were too heavy for them, found themselves 'volunteering' for the almost suicidal task of 'tank-busting' using a Panzerfaust, a light rocket launcher that didn't require accuracy. While the snipers could take cover in a building or among the rubble a hundred metres or more from their target, those armed with the lower-range weapon, the 30-metre rocket, were compelled to put themselves in the path of an oncoming tank and steady their aim as it rumbled towards them. Unless they were within range of the tank's machine gun, their missile was likely to bounce off the armour plating, so they had to hold their nerve until it was practically on top of them before firing. They wouldn't have time to run for cover, so they would have to throw themselves face down between the tracks and let several tons of screeching, lumbering metal roll over them, if the tank hadn't been immobilized by the exploding shell. Those fortunate enough to have been issued with the longer-range type often had time to take cover after firing their weapon, but the intensity of combat was traumatic and its effects on inexperienced young women can only be imagined.

It wasn't only the ferocity of the fighting that they had to endure, but the carnage. Few would have seen a dead body in their young lives until they were forced into the front line, so they were given a tour of the morgues to condition them to the sights they would be faced with in the final battle. What they saw there scared many for life. The mortuaries were full of dismembered corpses looking, as one girl remembered, like 'heaps of meat' and, perhaps worst of all, babies with their eyes wide open. But at least they weren't screaming. That horror still awaited them.

Child soldiers

For the Allies the prospect of fighting children was unthinkable. They had been trained to fire at the enemy without hesitation, but they couldn't think of these teenagers in those terms, although they were armed and programmed to kill.

THE AMERICANS HAD BEEN WARNED TO EXPECT RESISTANCE AND TOLD THEY WERE LIKELY TO BE FIRED ON BY BOYS AND GIRLS AS YOUNG AS EIGHT YEARS OLD

The first time American GIs encountered serious opposition from these young fanatics was at Aachen in autumn 1944. The city was a vital strategic point in the Siegfried Line, Germany's first line of defence, and its capture would be seen as a significant victory; the beginning of the end for the Third Reich.

For this reason, both sides poured in everything they could, fighting it out for three very long gruelling weeks during October, resulting in heavy casualties on both sides.

The American troops had been warned to expect fierce resistance and were told that they were likely to be fired upon by boys and girls as young as eight years old. But even though they were reminded that their weapons were as deadly as those fired by adult soldiers the GIs, some of whom were barely out of their teens themselves, could not envisage killing children. It was only after they had been fired upon by this ragtag army that they realized what had to be done if they were to conquer Germany and end the dictatorship.

Girls used as decoys

The 26th Infantry Regiment suffered a number of fatalities attributed to young female snipers in the streets of the city and though the Americans were sickened at the thought of having to kill underage soldiers, they were soon hardened after seeing their comrades bleeding out in the street. One of the snipers was believed to be around thirteen and though she had died after killing one of the platoon his friends felt 'demoralized' and guilty at having 'murdered' a child, although they vainly tried to reassure themselves that they had had no choice.

In another incident, the same platoon heard about a group of young defenders who had been crushed to death by one of their own tanks. After it had been knocked out, the GIs opened the hatch to find the dead crew were only boys and a single young girl.

At times Aachen's youthful defenders would resort to deadly games of tag with their adversaries, throwing bricks and stones at the Americans then running away in the hope of luring the GIs into a boobytrap or an ambush. A single anti-personnel mine loaded with ball bearings could kill half a dozen soldiers if they didn't spread out as they'd been trained to do. The Americans quickly learned that the Germans were using girls as decoys and decided that the only way to avoid being drawn into a trap was to use grenades or flamethrowers.

When these young 'werewolves' were captured their defiance would quickly dissolve as they asked for sweets and chocolate bars. They were children after all.

Female Nazi zealots

Military historian Tim Heath interviewed many female veterans of the fighting in Aachen and Berlin for his book *Hitler's Girls*, which he subtitled 'Doves Amongst Eagles', a tag line that belied the fanaticism and bloodlust which several of them displayed at the time.

Flak gunner Theresa Moelle described firing a four-barrelled Type-38 anti-aircraft gun at zero elevation against approaching Russians with barely concealed glee.

> 'It was an amazing and awe-inspiring site ... the tracer bullets streaked out like rain.'

She and the other young female members of the flak battery were hardly 'doves', but rather battle-hardened veterans who stood their ground against the relentless assault, refilling the magazines and loading them into the gun until they had run out of shells. Even then they didn't flee but stayed to disable the gun so that the Soviets couldn't use it.

They were typical of so many young Nazi zealots who believed fervently in their Führer and their destiny, which was to subjugate and enslave the 'inferior' races. They had vilified the Slavs as primitive *Untermenschen* and had given silent consent to the rape of Russia and the forced eviction, deportation and death of hundreds of thousands of its inhabitants. Many female Hitler fanatics facilitated those Aktions while others willingly participated in the atrocities or looked on approvingly from the sidelines. Now, in the final days of April 1945, they were anticipating fearful reprisals from an adversary they had fatally underestimated. The women had more to fear and it was perhaps for that reason that some of them found a desperate courage that their male comrades failed to display at that critical hour.

Violated by the victors

Theresa Moelle leapt into action when several soldiers and men of the *Volksstrum* took shelter from a Russian tank. She cursed them as she took aim with a Panzerfaust, hitting it in the sweet spot between the turret and the body. She recalls it exploding 'like a roman candle' and felt a 'momentary sense of total elation'. She was so euphoric and relieved that she jumped up and down waving her hands in the air, oblivious to the danger from Russian snipers and exploding shells.

Her celebration, however, was short-lived.

Five days later Hitler committed suicide in the bunker beneath the Reich Chancellery and on 2 May the guns fell silent. After almost two months of intense street fighting, Berlin was in Russian hands. And so too were its two million citizens, the majority of them women and children.

But even while the fighting still raged, German women – young and old alike – were raped and violated by Soviet soldiers. Few were spared. Thousands committed suicide rather than suffer the ordeal, others killed themselves because they could not live with the shame. It is estimated that between 95,000 and 130,000 women and girls were raped in Berlin alone, according to figures provided by the two main hospitals. In addition, there were countless victims who did not seek treatment, among them the Polish and Russian women who had been transported to Germany as slave labour. Those women who reported their ordeal to the Russian officers were invariably brushed off with a dismissive shrug or told they were lucky not to have been shot.

Brutality had been repaid with brutality. German and Austrian women accused their Soviet occupiers of war crimes and cursed them as 'beasts' and 'animals' in the familiar language of war. But vile as their behaviour undoubtedly had been, the blame surely lay with one man, the instigator of the most destructive conflict in history – Adolf Hitler. If it had not been for Hitler there would have been no rape of Berlin, no Stalingrad, no Auschwitz.

Conclusion

The women who took an active role in the Third Reich felt empowered, despite the retrogressive nature of the regime and Hitler's opposition to women in prominent positions and politics. Many of them were educated to a minimal level and shared a similar working-class background. Those who had received training held very basic qualifications in nursing and secretarial skills, so they viewed the possibility of joining the SS and the Wehrmacht in any capacity as an exciting opportunity. Furthermore, the Nazi education system actively discouraged intellectual attainment and academic excellence in all but spurious racial pseudo-science and fanciful Teutonic history, which meant that only those girls indoctrinated with Nazi ideology had a decent chance of employment in the system, although there were few genuine prospects for their advancement.

The competition for places had been significantly reduced by the regime's oppression of their political rivals in the Catholic Centre Party and the Social Democrats as well as the Communists, among whom were a large number of highly educated female activists. In addition, all Jewish women had been prohibited from attending universities and from participating in public life. If all of these women had not been taken out of the equation they would have offered their Nazi rivals formidable opposition, as they were not only well-educated, but highly politicized, having obtained the vote in 1919 as well as equal employment rights and access to higher education.

As it was, a generation of German women who were either ardent Nazis or sympathetic to the regime had gained an unprecedented advantage in securing employment. The women of the Third Reich felt them-selves to be among the privileged New Order, as well as valued members of the *Volksgemeinschaft* (people's community). As such, many attempted to justify their participation in genocide and other crimes by claiming that they were duty bound to comply with the collective popular will, which entertained no regard for individual conscience or morality.

As servants of a totalitarian state which had excluded itself from accepted standards of behaviour, and members of a self-proclaimed master race, they considered them-selves to be above the laws under which their inferiors lived and to be exempt from personal responsibility for their actions. However, in the wake of Germany's defeat, they discovered that the global community did not share their view and held them accountable under the concept known as collective guilt.

Under Hitler, his functionaries found themselves invested with unprecedented power over life and death and in turn the minor cogs in this murderous machine discovered that they would be largely unsupervised by or answerable to their superiors provided that they fulfilled their quotas and met the deadlines. Nobodies became somebodies overnight. Nonentities were rewarded for their zeal and slavish adherence to Party policy, while women were encouraged to bear children in preference to working on the production lines or educating the next generation and were awarded medals in recognition of their fecundity.

> ## UNDER HITLER FUNCTIONARIES WERE INVESTED WITH POWER OVER LIFE AND DEATH... NOBODIES BECAME SOMEBODIES OVERNIGHT

And what does this say about Gretl Braun, Gertrude Weisker and countless other young women who lived under Hitler in Nazi Germany?

It appears to challenge the enduring impression held by those who 'can't forgive and can't forget' that the Germans and their Austrian allies were a nation of rabid Nazis to a man (and woman) intent on following their Führer to self-destruction. True believers were certainly in the majority, as attested by the huge attendance at the Nuremberg rallies, but the general population must surely have been no more innately 'evil', or easily led than any other nation.

Gretl and her generation evidently succumbed to what amounted to a national psychosis induced by their pathological leader, a false messiah who exploited their suspicion of and antagonism towards the 'outsiders' in their midst; specifically the Jews, but also other minority groups. Hitler and his cronies then fanned these feelings into open hostility until they erupted in violence, intimidation and mass murder.

The majority of Germans also nurtured a barely suppressed hatred for their former enemies and a bitter resentment of those who had imposed punitive reparations on a defeated Germany after the humiliating defeat of 1918. This prepared them for the role of Hitler's willing accomplices and as such subject to the accusation of 'collective guilt', which subsequently gathered credence when countered by the conspiracy of denial that grew up to resist it. Almost a century after the founding of the National Socialist German Workers' Party in February 1920, the concept of collective temporary insanity must be considered objectively and the women of the Reich who did not take an active part in the persecution of the regime's enemies should be viewed as no different to their modern counterparts. They were possessed of the same flaws and failings and the same degree of self-absorption, but they were prey too to callous indifference and feelings of self-preservation, expressed by some as stubborn defiance and denial when forced to face the consequences of their actions or their failure to act when they might have made a difference. That perhaps, is the factor which distinguishes the women in the preceding pages from their modern counterparts, who still have the opportunity to make that choice.

Bibliography

Browning, Christopher *Ordinary Men* (Penguin, 2001)

Clancy, G.B. *Hitler's Lost Spy: The True Story of a Female Spy in Australia* (Sunda Publications, 2014)

Dillon, Christopher *Dachau and the SS* (Oxford University Press, 2016)

Eberle, Henrik (Ed.) *Letters to Hitler* (Polity, 2012)

Gutman, Israel *Encyclopedia of the Holocaust* (Macmillan, 1990)

Hagen, Louis *Nine Lives Under the Nazis* (The History Press, 2011)

Keun, Irmgard *The Artificial Silk Girl* (Neversink, 2011)

Keun, Irmgard *After Midnight* (Neversink, 2011)

Kilbourn, Russell and Ty, Eleanor *The Memory Effect* (Wilfrid Laurier University Press, 2013)

Kitterman, David H. *'Those Who Said No!'* (German Studies Review, May 1988)

Lelyveld, Joseph *Omaha Blues* (Picador, 2006)

Lucas, Richard *Axis Sally, The American Voice of Nazi Germany* (Casemate, 2010)

Mackinnon, Marianne *The Naked Years* (Corgi, 1989)

Maschmann, Melita *Account Rendered* (Plunkett Lake Press, 2013)

McKee, Ilse *Tomorrow the World* (Dent, 1960)

Milton, Giles *Fascinating Footnotes from History* (John Murray, 2015)

Newmann, Margarete *Under Two Dictators* (Pimlico, 2008)

Niemann, Derek *A Nazi in the Family* (Short Books, 2015)

Rashke, Richard *Useful Enemies* (Delphinium, 2013)

Sebba, Anne *Les Parisiennes* (St Martins Press, 2016)

Simkin, John Princess Stephanie article 'Spartacus-Educational.com' September 1997/April 2016

Setkiewicz, Piotr (Ed.) *The Private Lives of the Auschwitz SS* (Auschwitz Birkenau State Museum, 2014)

Spitz, Vivien *Doctors from Hell* (First Sentient, 2005)
Taylor, Frederick *Exorcising Hitler* (Bloomsbury, 2012)
Wachsmann, Nikolaus *KL: A History of the Nazi Concentration Camps* (Abacus, 2016)
Wilson, Jim *Nazi Princess: Hitler, Lord Rothermere and Princess Stephanie von Hohenlohe* (The History Press, 2011)
Wyden, Peter *Stella: One Woman's True Tale of Evil, Betrayal and Survival in Hitler's Germany* (Simon & Schuster, 1992)

Resources

A Nazi Past, a Queens Home Life, an Overlooked Death' *New York Times* (10 December 2005)
'I Was a Nazi and Here's Why' by Helen Epstein *The New Yorker* (May 2013)
adst.org (Association for Diplomatic Studies and Training)
ahrp.org
Chicago Tribune January 1993
coleshillhouse.com
Eyewintesstohistory.com
Historyextra.com
Historynet.com
John Simkin (spartacus-educational.com)
learning-from-history.de
marthahallkelly.com
mhpbooks.com
npr.org
nypost.com
Putschgirl.tumblr.com
spiegelonline.de
Theguardian.com
themillions.com
worldwartwo.filminspector.com

Index

After Midnight (Keun) 182–3
Albrecht, Mary 44
Arendt, Hannah 191
Artificial Silk Girl, The (Keun) 181–2
Axis Sally 103–5
Axmann, Artur 226

Bassler, Helga 226
Baur, Hans 27
BDM 183–6, 192–201
Beierl, Florian 12
Beimler, Centa 126
Beimler, Hans 126
Beinhorn, Elly 51
Benzinger, Theo 67–8
Bergmann, Gretel 57
Berlin Olympics 57–8, 101, 169
Bex, Hildegard 149
Bex, Renate 149
Bierganz, Maria 222–3
Bischoff, Hildegard 138
Bischoff, Karl 138
Bohnera, Karola 162
Bower, Tom 150, 151
Bradfisch, Otto 123
Braun, Eva
    relationship with Adolf Hitler
      18–19, 21–3, 24–8, 29
    physical description of 19–20
    suicide attempts 23–4
    marriage to Adolf Hitler 28
    memories of Gertrude Weisker
      29–30
Braun, Gretl
    physical description of 19–20
    first meeting with Adolf Hitler 20
    on Eva Braun's relationship with
      Hitler 21–3, 24–5, 26, 27
    on death of Eva Braun 28
Braun, Ilse 23, 28
Braun, Wernher von 53
Braunsteiner, Hermine 142–52
Breh, Albert 118
Brown, Eric 81–2
Brückner, Wilhelm 27, 41–2

Chamberlain, Neville 43, 92, 93,
    94, 103
Churchill, Winston 103
Cocteau, Jean 101

de Gaulle, Charles 131
de Gaulle, Geneviève 131
DeVito, Anthony 148, 152
Dietl, Eduard 102–3
Dubiel, Stanislaw 161
Duquesne, Frederick 98
Eberstein, Ernst 50
Eckermann, Kirsten 196
Epstein, Helen 187
Etzdorf, Marga von 51, 55
Eucker, Wilhelm K. 34
Eva's Cousin (Knauss) 30

F., Anneliese 116–17
Fischer, Dr 134, 136, 139
Fritzch, Karl 160
Fromm, Bella 94

Gartner, Marianne 168–78
Gebhardt, Karl 133, 136
Gelmo, Paul 132
German Woman, The (Walter) 37–8
German Women's Bureau 117
German Women's Order 34–5
Gillars, Mildred 103–5
Goebbels, Joseph 75, 77, 101, 174,
    221, 223
Goebbels, Magda 77
Goebel, Franz 166
Goering, Emmy 66
Goering, Hermann 58, 62, 63, 66–7,
    70, 72, 75, 76, 92, 93
Goeth, Amon 161
Goldschlag, Gerhard 107–8
Goldschlag, Stella 105–12
Goldschlag, Toni 109
Goldschmidt, Leonore 108
Grant, Linda 29, 30
Greim, Robert Ritter von 75–6, 77,
    78, 80, 82

Hagen, Louis 209–10
Halifax, Lord 93
Hammond Jr., Ogden H. 98
Hanfstaengl, Ernst 86
Hannecker, Gertrude 101
Hansen, Frau 176
Harding, Thomas 163
Heath, Tim 197, 199, 229
Heidorn, Georg 220, 221
Heimerdinger, Ilse 207
Henneman, Karl-Heinz 220, 221
Hess, Rudolf 35, 36
Hesse, Susanne 41
Heydrich, Reinhard 132–3
Himmler, Heinrich 67, 70,
    74, 75, 78, 87, 101, 115, 126, 131,
    133, 139, 158, 205, 210
Hirsch, Ilse 217–22
Hitler, Adolf
    forged diaries 12
    childhood of 13–15
    in Vienna 25
    reunion with Paula Hitler 16
    relationship with Eva Braun 18–19,
        21–3, 24–8, 29
    support from women 31–4, 35–6,
        37–40, 42–3, 44–5
    rise to power 36–7
    appeals for help from women 39–42
    and Berlin Olympics 57
    reaction to Operation Suicide 69–70
    assassination attempt on 70–2
    final days in Berlin bunker 74–8
    fears over Stephanie Julienne
        Richter's Jewishness 86–7
    meets Stephanie Julienne Richter
        87–8
    relationship with Stephanie Julienne
        Richter 88, 89–90, 94–5
    and Violette Morris 102
Hitler, Alois (father of Adolf Hitler)
    12, 13–14
Hitler, Alois (half-brother of Adolf
    Hitler) 12
Hitler, Angela 12, 42
Hitler, Paula

childhood of 12, 13, 14
diaries of 12–13
interviewed 13–14
reunion with Adolf Hitler 16
knowledge of Nazi atrocities 16–17
Hitler's Furies (Lower) 121
Hitler's Girls (Heath) 197, 229
Hodys, Eleanor 162
Hoess, Brigitte 157–65
Hoess, Hedwig 158, 159, 160–1, 162
Hoess, Rudolf 157, 158–9, 162, 164–5
Hoffmann, Erna 23
Hoffmann, Heinrich 20, 22, 23, 25, 66
Hoffmann, Henriette 27
Hohenlohe, Franz 96
Hohenlohe-Waldenburg Schillingsfürst,
    Friedrich Franz von 87
Hoover, J. Edgar 95–6
Horning, Klaus 122–3
Huber, Irmgard 213, 215–16
Hummel, Maria Innocentia 166

Irrgang, Frau 43
Isaacsohn, Rolf 110

Jaeger, George 213–14
Jekelius, Erwin 13
Junge, Traudl 33, 77

K., Annelene 40–1
Karolewska, Vladislava 134–6
Kaus, Gina 87
Keun, Irmgard 181–3
Kitterman, David H. 123
KL: A History of the Nazi
    Concentration Camp (Wachsmann)
    161
Klein, Alphons 213, 216
Knauss, Sibylle 32
Kneissler, Pauline 216–17
Koegel, Anna 165–6
Koegel, Max 165, 166
Krappot, Fräulein 139
Kubizek, August 15
Kubler, Manfred 108
Kujau, Konrad 12

Kurunda, Ludmilla 87
Kuttner, Joachim 83

Lange, Heinrich 67–8
League of German Maidens (BDM)
    183–6, 192–201
Lee, Marina 102–3
Leitgeb, Joseph 220
Lelyveld, Joseph 142–3, 144, 145,
    146, 148
Lichtenburg concentration camp
    126–7
Lindbergh, Charles 57
Lippert, Marie 117
Lippert, Michael 117
Lot, Maître 100
Lower, Wendy 121
Ludolph, Erna 127

Mangert, Herr 175
Maschmann, Melita 183–91
Mauriac, François 127
Mayer, Helene 57
Mein Kampf 15, 36, 38, 39
Menzel, Elsa 42
Menzel, Paul 42
Menzies, Robert Gordon 114
Merkle, Adolph 215
Milch, Erhard 69
Mitford sisters 89, 90
Moelle, Theresa 229, 230
Morgenschweiss, Erich 220, 221
Moringen concentration camp 126
Morris, Violette 99–102
Muller, Franz 116–17
Munich Agreement 43–4
National Socialist Women's League 35

Neumann, Margarete Buber 128–30
New York Times 96
Niemann, Anna–Luise 155
Niemann, Dieter 157
Niemann, Eckart Josef 156, 157
Niemann, Karl 154–5, 156–7
Niemann, Minna 154–7
Nogler, Friede 45–6

Oberheuser, Herta 132–7
Oberhummer, Maria 44
Oesterle, Julie 43
Opitz, Paul 72
Oppenhoff, Franz 218–19, 220–2
Ostermeyer, Herta 22

Pawela, Maria 138
Prützmann, Hans-Adolf 219

R., Ingeborg 118
RAD (Reich Labour Service) 201–2
Rathmann, Margarthe 36
Raubal, Geli 20–1, 25
Ravensbrück concentration camp
    127–37, 139–40, 147, 165–6
Reinhardt, Max 92
Reitsch, Hanna
    description of 48–9
    early life and career 50
    rivalry with Melitta von
        Stauffenberg 50, 56, 64, 68
    trains as pilot 52–3
    support for Adolf Hitler 53
    gliding accident 54
    tests gliders 56
    presented with pilot's badge 58
    as military test pilot 59, 60–2
    awarded Iron Cross 62, 65, 69
    sexuality of 64
    crashes in rocket–powered plane 64
    concerns over war 66–9
    plans Operation Suicide 68–70, 73
    tour of Eastern Front 69
    loyalty to Nazis 73–4, 80–2
    in Berlin bunker 74–8
    interrogation after war 81–3
    writes memoirs 84
Richter, Stephanie Julienne
    noble title 85
    Jewish background checked 86–7
    meets Adolf Hitler 87–8
    relationship with Hitler 88, 89–90
    acts on behalf of Nazis 90–5
    internment 95–6
    death of 96

Riedel, Peter 64, 74
Roehm, Ernst 101
Rogoff, Guenther 109
Rothermere, Lord 91–3, 94, 95
Ryan, Hermine 142–52
Ryan, Russell 145, 148
Ryback, Timothy 12

Salvator, Franz 87
Samuelson, Arthur 191
Schaller, Ingeborg 201–2
Schirach, Baldur von 98
Schneider, Walter H. 139
Scholtz-Klink, Gertrud 35
Schönmann, Marion 23
Schoener, Anita von 198–9
Scholl, Sophie 199–200
Schwanenflügel, Dorothea von 193–4
Schwarzhuber, Johann 161
Schweitzer, Marianne 187–8, 189–90
Sebold, William 99
Selby, Walford 94
Skorzeny, Otto 64, 74
Sledziejowska-Osiczko,
Stanislawa 134
Snowdon, Lady 93
Spacil, Josef 155
Speer, Albert 27, 75
Stauffenberg, Alexander von 51–2,
    72, 78–9
Stauffenberg, Claus von 70–1, 72
Stauffenberg, Melitta von
    description of 48–9
    early life and career 49–50
    rivalry with Hanna Reitsch 50, 56,
    64, 68
    trains as pilot 50–1
    marriage 51–2
    dislike of Nazis 55
    research work 55–6, 58–9
    at Berlin Olympics 58 as test pilot
    59–60, 62–4, 72–3
    awarded Iron Cross 66
    assassination attempt on Hitler 70–1
    imprisonment 72
    visits family in concentration camp

78–9
    death of 79–80
    courage of 84
Stawarczyk, Aleksandra 139
Stein, Lilly 98–9
Stoffl, Anna 94
Streszak, Lieselotte 109–10
Stroh, Helga 197
Suhren, Elfriede 166
Suhren, Fritz 165, 166

Those Who Said No! (Kitterman) 123
Tillion, Germaine 128
Toland, John 20, 27
Trapp, Major 121
Trommel, Dr 135–6
Trutz, Ernst 209
Trutz, Hildegard 203–7, 208–10

Udet, Ernst 50, 60, 62
Under Two Dictators (Neumann) 129

Voggesberger, Cazilie 117–18
Voggesberger, Josef 117–18
Vollmer, Herbert 118

Wachsmann, Nikolaus 161
Wagner, Annette 112–14
Wagner, Robert 113
Wagner, Winifred 21
Wahlmann, Adolf 216
Walter, Elsa 37–8, 39
Weiner, Max 87
Weisker, Gertrude 29–30
Wenzel, Herbert 220, 221
Wessel, Horst 41
Wiedemann, Fritz 87, 92, 94–5
Wiesenthal, Simon 143, 145, 149
Wijk, Gerth van 102
Witek, Prakseda 138
Wohlauf, Julius 120, 121
Wohlauf, Vera 119–22
Work, Robert 82
Wyden, Peter 108, 109, 111–12

Zander, Elspeth 34–5